'Hindus and non-Hindus alike caution us that Hinduism defies every definition of the term "religion." How then to lay out its basics? Yet Neelima Shukla-Bhatt does just that, skillfully relating major concepts and moments of historical evolution to the everyday practices of Hindus around the world. Gender and social station get special attention. It's a triumph!'

John Stratton Hawley, *Columbia University, USA*

'An extraordinary achievement! Neelima Shukla-Bhatt has written an easy-to-read introduction to a continuous and complex, ancient and modern religious tradition. She enables us to see Hinduism grounded in daily life and religious practice while also introducing us to the wide range of sacred texts and the multitude of gods. Here readers will encounter a vibrant religious tradition.'

Diana L. Eck, *Harvard University, USA*

HINDUISM

THE BASICS

Hinduism: The Basics introduces readers to the third largest, and arguably the oldest, living religious tradition. It opens a vista into the rich and dynamic ethos of the Hindu religious tradition in India and other parts of the world. The book explores the variety of philosophical schools, priestly rituals, and popular practices common in the Hindu faith, presenting the layered diversity of its traditions and how they function in everyday life.

Chapters unpack key concepts from the tradition and discussions about its various aspects, including:

- The historical development of Hinduism
- Religious practices such as pilgrimage, meditation, and life cycle rituals
- The organisation of Hindu society into castes and related social justice issues
- The continuum between sacred texts in elite Sanskrit and in South Asian vernacular languages
- Hindu worldviews including karma, reincarnation, and ethics
- The spread of Hinduism around the world, the rise of Hindu nationalism, and other challenges of modernity
- The vitality of indigenous cultures in every form of Hinduism

Featuring glossaries, timelines, suggestions for further reading, and a list of key deities as well as practices, this is an ideal introduction to Hindu beliefs and traditions for undergraduates and others new to the study of Hinduism.

Neelima Shukla-Bhatt is a Professor of Religion at Wellesley College, Wellesley, USA.

THE BASICS

The Basics is a highly successful series of accessible guidebooks which provide an overview of the fundamental principles of a subject area in a jargon-free and undaunting format.

Intended for students approaching a subject for the first time, the books both introduce the essentials of a subject and provide an ideal springboard for further study. With over 50 titles spanning subjects from artificial intelligence (AI) to women's studies, *The Basics* are an ideal starting point for students seeking to understand a subject area.

Each text comes with recommendations for further study and gradually introduces the complexities and nuances within a subject.

For more information about this series, please visit: www.routledge.com/The-Basics/book-series/B

HINDUISM

THE BASICS

Neelima Shukla-Bhatt

Routledge
Taylor & Francis Group

LONDON AND NEW YORK

Designed cover image: © Getty Images

First published 2023
by Routledge
4 Park Square, Milton Park, Abingdon, Oxon OX14 4RN

and by Routledge
605 Third Avenue, New York, NY 10158

Routledge is an imprint of the Taylor & Francis Group, an informa business

© 2023 Neelima Shukla-Bhatt

British Library Cataloguing-in-Publication Data
A catalogue record for this book is available from the British Library

Library of Congress Cataloging-in-Publication Data
Names: Shukla-Bhatt, Neelima, author.
Title: Hinduism : the basics / Neelima Shukla-Bhatt.
Description: 1. | New York : Routledge, 2023. | Series: The basics ; book 185 | Includes bibliographical references and index.
Identifiers: LCCN 2022042322 | ISBN 9780415716451 (hardback) | ISBN 9780415716468 (paperback) | ISBN 9781315303352 (ebook)
Subjects: LCSH: Hinduism.
Classification: LCC BL1202 .S398 2023 | DDC 294.5--dc23/eng/20220902
LC record available at https://lccn.loc.gov/2022042322

ISBN: 978-0-415-71645-1 (hbk)
ISBN: 978-0-415-71646-8 (pbk)
ISBN: 978-1-315-30335-2 (ebk)

DOI: 10.4324/9781315303352

Typeset in Bembo
by KnowledgeWorks Global Ltd.

For
all peace-lovers in the world
Prithvi Shanti!

CONTENTS

LIST OF FIGURES

PREFACE

This book has been long in the making. There are already several excellent Introductions to Hinduism. The question my editors and I kept in view in thinking about it was: What could this short book distinctively offer? I found clues to the answer in a few different ways. First, questions of my students from all parts of the world at Wellesley College directed me to themes and issues in which young people are widely interested. Second, many conversations with young Hindus in the United States and India provided pointers to what they seek to understand about their cultural background whether or not they identify as religious. Third, questions of participants in a number of interfaith events helped me discern patterns of general inquiry about the Hindu tradition and culture. Fourth, and importantly, emails of several young, and not so young students from around the globe in my online HarvardX course "Hinduism through its Scriptures" with enrollment of more than 150,000 over the past few years, energized me to find ways to integrate themes that would answer their queries. I had the privilege to grow up in villages, small towns, and cosmopolitan cities in western India allowing me to interact closely with people in diverse contexts. I then had the benefit to study and be a part of academia in the USA. I realized that what I can bring to a book like this is a focus on religious lives of average rural and urban Hindus for whom religion is not necessarily a search for an exalted transcendental experience, but a thread woven in their daily routine and special days that makes them deeply meaningful. In this book, many examples are drawn from lives of people of non-elite backgrounds who form a large majority of the Hindu society and many of whom are underprivileged. A major core of this book is the basics of their religious life. The book, however, does not ignore the religion's foundational aspects drawn from ancient Sanskrit texts including mystical insights related to spiritual practices like yoga. It rather draws attention to the ways in which components derived from Sanskrit and vernacular sacred texts, regional tribal cultures, and diverse historical developments are simultaneously at work in the lives of ordinary Hindus. Its orientation is descriptive. The book is presented for interested readers in the hope that it will throw light on some discernible patterns of an immensely diverse and complex religious tradition with ancient roots.

ACKNOWLEDGMENTS

As is widely acknowledged, no book is the fruit of the labor of a single individual. This book is no exception. I am indebted to the innumerable Hindu and non-Hindu individuals who freely shared their views and experiences with me. I am also deeply grateful to Guru Krupa Foundation (GKF), New York, for their generous financial support for the research for this book. The book could not have been completed without the support of four academic institutions. My home institution, Wellesley College, generously offered me funds and time needed for research. With its hospitality and generous support in all aspects of the project during the critical phases of both research and writing, FLAME University, Pune, India, became my second intellectual home. The Bhandarkar Oriental Institute, Pune, and the Delhi office of American Institute of Indian Studies allowed me access to their rich libraries and archives during research. I am immensely thankful for all these institutions for their help. I also thank my friends and family without whose care I could not have overcome the hurdles, especially those related to COVID, in writing. Finally, I sincerely express my gratitude to the most supportive and patient editorial team of Taylor & Francis who were never tired of helping me as I gave the book its present shape. Any shortcomings in the book are mine alone.

NOTE ON TRANSLITERATION AND ABBREVIATIONS

In this work, special characters and abbreviations are used sparingly. The words that are found in English dictionaries (such as "Purana" and "Upanishads") are used in their standardized forms. The names of persons, deities, and mythical characters (Shiva, Krishna, Durga, etc.), communities (Warkari), and actual or mythical places (Vrindavan, Pune, etc.) are also used in their commonly found forms in English-language texts.

Titles of well-known texts are italicized but without special characters. Words and quotes in Sanskrit and other Indic languages are in italics and transliterated according to the standard system.

- The long vowels – *ā, ī,* and *ū* – are pronounced approximately like vowels in "c*a*lm," "b*ee*," and "c*oo*l," respectively.
- Retroflex consonants – *ṭ, ṭh, ḍ, ṇ* – found in many Indian languages but having no English equivalents are indicated with a dot underneath.
- The two sibilants, *ś* and *ṣ* – both pronounced like English "*sh*" – are indicated as different following spellings in Indian languages.

Abbreviations are used only for the titles of well-known ancient Sanskrit texts – *Rig Veda* – RV, *Sama Veda* – SV, *Yajur Veda* – YV, *Atharva Veda* – AV, and *Bhagavad Gita* – BG.

INTRODUCTION

A RIVER AND A RELIGION

A book titled *Hinduism, the Basics* must necessarily start by specifying how it defines "Hinduism" and in what sense the aspects discussed here are basic to it. So, let's start with the "-ism" part. The entry for suffix "-ism" in the Oxford English dictionary lists five different ways in which it forms nouns that denote: (a) action, (b) a state, (c) a system, principle or ideological movement, (d) bias, and (e) a peculiarity in language. Of these, the use of "-ism" that is apparently relevant to the term "Hinduism" is denoting a "system." But what kind of system? The suffix is used in words denoting several religious and spiritual traditions. In terms such as "Buddhism," and "Confucianism," it is added to the name or the title of the founder whose teachings form the foundations of the tradition. In the term "Taoism," it is added to a word denoting a concept (Tao – "the way"). But in the terms "Judaism," and "Hinduism," signifying two of the oldest religious traditions of the world spanning over three millennia, it is added to base words that refer to geographical areas rather than founders or sets of concepts.

How does a geographical area provide the basis of a system? In the case of "Judaism," the base word refers to the ancient Judea

DOI: 10.4324/9781315303352-1

region (in the present-day Israel). With the addition of "-ism," the term denotes the monotheistic religion that initially developed among ethnic groups living in and around it. Some Jewish scholars point out however that in its early usage, the Greek term from which the term "Judaism" is derived meant the totality of the cultural characteristics of Judaean people of which religious beliefs and practices were a part. The base word for "Hinduism" – "Hindu" – as first used centuries before the Common Era by ancient Persians, referred to the area or people living in the east of the river "Sindhu" (the "Indus," also the origin of the term/name "India"). In early works by visitors to India, we find a portrayal of diverse aspects of the life of the "Hindu" people (*Indoi* in Greek) and not just religion. Such a portrayal is largely relevant even today since it is difficult to distinguish between exclusively religious and purely cultural practices of Hindus.

Long after the ancient usage of the term "Hindu," in the early nineteenth century, the term "Hinduism" began to be used widely in the English language to connote a religious system. What it gradually came to signify for both outsiders and insiders is a network of diverse but overlapping beliefs and practices of a large majority of people in India who were not followers of Abrahamic religions or of Indic religious traditions that were identified as distinct – Jainism, Buddhism, and Sikhism. "Judaism" and "Hinduism" are thus terms connoting religious traditions that developed ethno-geographically and remain linked to a considerable extent to the cultures of the people in the areas where they originated. But beyond the ethno-geographical nature of their evolution, the two traditions are vastly different. Even with its internal diversity, strict monotheism forms the core of all branches of Judaism, whereas Hinduism defies attempts to define a single unchanging core belief.

There is no dogma or practice that is embraced uniformly by all of the one billion plus people in the world who identify as Hindu today. Nor can its origins be traced to a single figure, text, or doctrine. There is also no centralized religious authority or institution for Hindus. Hinduism is immensely diverse and fluid in both beliefs and practices. Some Hindus believe that the divine is without form and attributes; some worship various deities with form who make a large pantheon – Shiva, Vishnu, the great goddess, Krishna, Rama, Ganesha, etc.; and some worship a single deity. Some may even be atheists. Some regularly perform worship rituals for images of the deities; some may sing hymns; some may practice only meditation; and some may see serving others as the way to follow their religion. Some may study and chant mantras from ancient texts in the Sanskrit language; many may not even know the titles of those texts. Because of the innumerable forms of worship and beliefs, often with no singular formal religious institution, Hinduism is extremely difficult to define.

How do we begin to understand the basics of such a tradition? Here, the integral link of a river to the naming of "Hinduism" offers a nice opening. The river Sindhu flows over 2,000 miles from its source in the Tibetan plateau, growing larger as tributaries converge into it from its east and west, sometimes turbulent and sometimes tranquil, sometimes narrow and sometimes like a vast sea, passing through varied landscapes, and changing its course at times. It nourishes diverse life forms and makes fertile the land through which it flows. Like its namesake river, "Hinduism" as we know it today, has been developing for over 3,000 years with numerous religious and cultural currents converging to form an enormous flow of tradition. This flow has been shaped by innumerable individuals and interactions with different cultures; has grown with numerous streams of interpretations; has different forms region to region; offers spiritual sustenance to millions of people; has had its floods and turbulences; but has continued to move on in history. It is prevalent today as the majority religion in India and Nepal within South Asia, Mauritius in the Indian ocean, and in the province of Bali in Indonesia. It is a minority religion in many other parts of the world. Despite the absence of a single founder or a dogma embraced by all Hindus, the network of Hinduism has remained woven together to a considerable extent because a large majority of its adherents focus on ways to tap into the sacred power of the cosmos for both worldly lives and inner transformation. Divinities, sacred groves, trees, rivers are seen by Hindus as manifesting that power and religious practices provide doors into it. This feature, along with some widely accepted spiritual concepts, moral values, and goals for human life hold together the linked group of traditions that we know as "Hinduism." In this book, we will consider important currents of thought and practices that have contributed to shaping Hinduism as practiced by millions of Hindus today. We will traverse through millennia of history and diverse lands within and outside India. In exploring various aspects of the tradition, we will not look simply at the elite thought and practices, but a major focus for us will remain on non-elite and regional texts and practices in which lives of average Hindus are embedded.

AN ORDINARY AND A SPECIAL DAY IN THE LIFE OF A HINDU FAMILY

Let us begin our journey not in antiquity in search of elusive origins of Hinduism, but with snapshots of the likely daily routine of a contemporary middle-class Hindu family living on the outskirts of the city of Pune in western India and their activities on a special day. Even though the names used here are imaginary, the snapshots are based on real-life practices. We will call this imaginary family, whom we will keep meeting from time to time in the book, the Kulkarnis.

It is 6:30 in the morning on a day in the month of June. The stir of activities in the Kulkarni household has already started. The lady of the house, Rukma, has taken her bath. She picks up a two-bowl tray filled with white and red powders, steps out of the house, and within minutes makes a floral design with auspicious symbols near the door and on the threshold, softly singing her favorite hymn in her mother-tongue Marathi. The act of making the design while half-audibly singing a hymn is Rukma's first prayer of the day to mother earth and to the great goddess to bless with good fortune her home and everyone who enters it (Figure 0.1).

It is also her gesture to welcome guests into her home. Each day, she completes this ritual immediately after her bath and then gets busy with preparing breakfast and lunch for the family before she leaves at 9:00 for work. She sees them as her wifely and motherly duties and often refers to them as her *dharma*.

The design made by Rukma is called *rāṅgoḷī* in her part of India. But similar designs in front of the house or on the walls made by

Figure 0.1 A woman making *rāngoḷī* at the entrance of her home.
Photograph by the author.

women with a variety of materials are found all over the country and have different regional names (*rangolī* in north India, *muggu* in Andhra, *alpanā* in Bengal, *kolam* in Tamil Nadu, etc.). In my native region, Gujarat, it is called *sāthiyo* (plu. *sāthiyā*). One of my fond memories of my grandmother is when she learned that our family in the city had stopped making *sāthiyā* in the morning. She joked that we had become uncivilized since we no longer cared to warmly welcome guests or offer a prayer to mother earth by creating something beautiful in the front of our house each day. Rukma too shares such a view of the practice with millions of women in India.

Rukma's husband Govind will get up at 7:30, take his morning tea prepared by her, and read the newspaper before taking his bath. After bath, he will sit in front of a small wooden shrine in a corner of the kitchen and offer daily ritual worship – *pūjā* – to small images of four deities in that shrine – Krishna, Shiva, Ganesha, and the goddess. He will wash them, put sandalwood marks on them, put flower petals on them, light a lamp, wave it around the images, and finally offer crystals of sugar as food offering (*prasād*), all the while chanting verses (*ślokas*) from ancient texts called the Vedas and from the famous Hindu text the *Bhagavad Gita (BG)*. He works for a bank and will leave home around 10:00. On his way, he will stop at a large temple for five minutes, have a viewing (*darśan*) of the image of Ganesha, and greet the priest. At 8:00, Rukma's college-going children, son Ravi and her daughter Chaitrali, will get up. By 8:30 their household help, Manju, from the adjacent village will arrive. Manju belongs to a different community from Rukma's family, which is lower in the hereditary and hierarchical Hindu social organization, generally known as the "caste system" (about which we will learn later in greater detail). She will help Chaitrali prepare coffee, and the three – Ravi, Chaitrali, and Manju – will have it. The children will leave at 10:30 for their summer courses. Ravi generally bows to the deities in the family shrine before leaving; Chaitrali does not.

Manju will then clean up the kitchen, wash clothes, lock the house, and then leave. On her way back home, she will stop and offer flowers at a small shrine on the roadside that has no priest. The deity there is the protective goddess of her village. The narrative about the temple is that the goddess appeared in the dream of a villager and asked him to dig near the village lake. When he did so, he found the image of the goddess. The goddess again appeared in his dream and promised to protect the village. People in Manju's neighborhood collected a small amount of money and built the shrine where the image was found. They visit the shrine daily and offer flowers. Not many people from upper castes visited the goddess shrine until recently. They only bowed their heads slightly when passing by the shrine. With the growing reputation of the goddess for her healing powers, however, village residents belonging to all castes are now collecting funds for a bigger temple. They agree it is their collective *dharma* to honor the goddess of their village.

In the evening, Rukma will return from work around 6:00. She will finish cooking by 7:00 and then light a lamp by the basil plant in front of the house. When returning home from work, Govind will visit his old parents in the city with groceries they need. In this, he will perform his *dharma* as their son. From 6:00 to 7:00 in the evening, Ravi will go to a class on the *Bhagavad Gita*, the well-known Hindu sacred text in Sanskrit. The class is taught by a female guru ordained in a major spiritual lineage. Chaitrali will come home at 5:00 and then go to Manju's neighborhood where she teaches young children dances based on Hindu narratives for the festival of Ganesha that generally falls in September. She will first greet the children in their families, folding hands and saying *Namaste*, the Hindu greeting meaning "I bow to (the divine presence within) you." This is an everyday expression for recognizing the presence of the Ultimate in all existence, a concept we will consider later. Chaitrali sees serving the underprivileged as the most dharmic thing to do. She will return home with Manju at 7:00 p.m. The family will have their dinner together in the dining area. Manju will have her dinner as well; but she will eat separately. She will clean the dishes by 8:30. Generally, she goes back home after that. But tonight, she will stay back to help Rukma with special preparations for tomorrow.

Tomorrow is a big day. A large number of pilgrims performing a yearly regional pilgrimage called Wari will pass through Pune. They are called Warkaris and include men and women from all strata of the society. They walk in groups called *dindi*s for over 100 miles from the nearby village of Dehu to Pandharpur (the site of Lord Vishnu's incarnation as Vitthala). The Warkaris in each *ḍiṇḍi* from Dehu carry a palanquin with the image of the seventeenth-century Marathi saint and poet Tukaram (Figure 0.2).

Figure 0.2 Warkaris walking and a first-aid Stall, Pune, Maharashtra, June 2019.
Photograph by the author.

Another major Wari from the village of Alandi with a palanquin carries the image of the thirteenth-century saint-poet Jnaneshwar who wrote a poetic commentary in the regional Marathi language on the *Bhagavad Gita*, the text Ravi studies in the evenings. For Warkaris, rather than ancient Sanskrit scriptures, lyrics of saintly poets of their region form the most important religious texts. The Warkaris sing these lyrics as songs throughout the pilgrimage. On the third and fourth days of this pilgrimage, as Wari pilgrims pass through the city of Pune, the city residents set up stalls to offer them food, water, medicines, and other necessary things for the journey. Rukma's family and two other families from their neighborhood will set up a stall on a nearby street. Tonight, Rukma will make her specialty *rava laddoo* (a sweet treat) in bulk. Manju will help and join the family at the stall tomorrow. They will place all *laddoo*s in front of the family shrine for a few minutes to get them blessed by the deities. Then Chaitrali and Ravi will pack the *laddoo*s in polythene bags. Rukma's neighbor Roma, who is from Bengal in eastern India, is making a snack called *nimki* from that region and is excited to be a part of a tradition of western India. The third family is getting bottles of water. Most businesses in the city will be closed tomorrow. Govind and the men in the other families will drive the group to a nearby spot on the route. The families will set up their stall by 7:30 in the morning, offer bags of food and water bottles to the Warkaris till 4:00 pm, and enjoy their devotional songs as they pass by. The next day will be another routine day.

Manju enjoys doing the stall activities every year. It is an open atmosphere where people interact with ease, unlike some other places where she feels discriminated against as a lower caste woman. The lyrics of saint-poets sung by the Warkaris express deep devotion to Vitthala; but convey a disregard for caste hierarchies. Manju feels like an equal participant in the community activities at the stall. Another time she had felt similarly was while taking a dip in the Ganga river when she had accompanied the Kulkarnis on a pilgrimage to Haridwar in the foothills of the Himalayas to help take care of their parents on the journey. She feels comfortable with the Kulkarnis. She thinks they treat her like family and has worked for them for several years. Her husband, however, keeps a distance from them since he belongs to a group deeply critical of hierarchies based on caste or economic class. Still he does not interfere with his wife's warm relationship with the Kulkarnis or her participation in the stall activities, which has been her yearly routine for long.

The Kulkarnis and Manju, like a large number of Hindu families, are not formally affiliated with any specific sect, even though some of their friends are. Rukma and Govind frequently attend lectures on spiritual teachings by a well-regarded monk whom they call *gurujī*. However, they are not his disciples formally. As a family, the Kulkarnis share some experiences such as organizing a stall for the Warkari pilgrims. They have a broader sense of sharing when taking a dip in the river Ganga at Haridwar where Hindu pilgrims from all over the country are seen. But in general, each person in the family connects to what she/he views as the sacred in a different way. Everyone incorporates in his/her routine some religious element that speaks to them. Each of these elements has its source in a different layer of the Hindu tradition ranging from ancient sacred texts in Sanskrit to regional folk narratives. Acceptance of diverse approaches and multiple textual sources for connecting with the sacred is normal in their religious culture. This makes it difficult to precisely define the core of their religion, Hinduism. And yet, it is possible to trace the evolution of the term from the layers of history since antiquity.

PORTRAYAL AND FRAMING OF THE "HINDU" WORLD

As mentioned earlier, ancient Persians referred to the region and people living east of the river Sindhu as Hindu. Their suit was followed by ancient Greeks who visited India after its invasion by Alexander the Great. They called Indians *Indoi*. In their accounts, diversity of Indian communities and their modes of life are mentioned but the term is not affiliated with a specific religion. A few centuries later, Xuan-Zang (seventh-century CE), the Chinese pilgrim who visited India to study Buddhist texts and moral teachings (*dhamma*, from "dharma"), called the land *In-tu*. In his writings, he describes diverse Buddhist schools in India and their debates with other schools of religious thought including those we now identify as "Hindu." Additionally, he describes various castes in India; but does not associate them with any specific religion. Even with rigorous debates and rivalry for patronage among philosophical schools, the general cultural/religious ethos seems to have been fluid at the time.

It is in the second millennium, in the writings of Al-Beruni, a scholar companion of Mahmud of Ghazni who invaded India in the eleventh century, that we first begin to get the portrayal of a religious ethos with distinctive markers that are associated with Hinduism today. Using the term "Hindu," Al-Beruni dispassionately recorded the thought and customs of people he encountered in India and found them to be completely different from those of his own religion – Islam. Thus, it is through a comparison to a monotheistic tradition that a distinct sense of "Hindu" religious culture associated with India (*al-Hind*) begins to emerge. Scholars of religion have shown that in the centuries that followed, a notion of a distinct religious culture that later came to be known as Hinduism had begun to evolve in India in different ways. Andrew Nicholson has discussed how some philosophers from the twelfth through the sixteenth centuries within India traced a unified and distinctly identifiable school of metaphysical thought from selected Sanskrit texts that are now associated with Hinduism. Diana Eck has shown that pilgrims to sites associated with various deities in Hindu mythology created pilgrimage circuits from which a picture of a distinct sacred landscape belonging to a religious community arises. David Lorenzen has demonstrated that in the centuries following Al-Beruni, when many people had converted to Islam and several parts of India had Muslim rulers, comparative references to the ways of the "Hindus" and the "Turks" (an ethnic term often used for Muslims during the time) were commonly found in writings in Indic languages including lyrics of regional saint-poets. They refer to two different religious cultures with Brahmins and Mullahs (Hindu and Muslim clerics) as their elites. A broad notion of a widely spread religious culture in India referenced as "Hindu" was prevalent; but it was not thought of exactly as a well-structured system or "-ism."

It was only in the nineteenth century that the specific term "Hinduism" connoting a cohesive religious system came to be used widely by English language publications in India and elsewhere. Even though its first usage in print is found in two writings of Hindu thinker Ram Mohan Roy in 1816–1817, it was not a common term used by Indians until after its widespread use in the English language in the nineteenth century. Only gradually, it began to be used by Hindus themselves. A need to place varied yet intersecting religious currents within an overarching system was recognized as important by both groups from different perspectives and with distinct incentives. It was a time when the term "religion," with connotations that had evolved in Europe since the enlightenment had been brought to European colonies. With India being a major part of the British empire, the overarching category of "Hinduism" was helpful in classifying its subjects. On their part, educated Indians who studied in the British-established institutions also welcomed the nomenclature of "religion" for their sacred practices and beliefs as a way to articulate a collective identity. For 200 years now, the term "Hinduism" has been in use. It is, however, seen as problematic by some people on two grounds. First, it is not an indigenous term; and second, the culture of interrelated religious currents it denotes does not exactly fit the western understanding of "religion." Many scholars today prefer the term "Hindu traditions" in plural to indicate the multiplicity of currents within this cluster. However, in this book the term "Hinduism" is used in its general sense to refer to the network of overlapping but diverse religious traditions.

As the above overview indicates, the term "Hinduism" has gradually evolved over two millennia since the ancient use of the term "Hindu" by outsiders. This leads to the ostensive question: What term or terms did Hindus use for themselves or their tradition until the term began to be used widely? Historically, adherents of various Hindu religious paths in different contexts have identified themselves by distinctive terms that generally refer to some aspect of their belief or practice. In ancient times followers of the ancient texts – the Vedas – called their tradition Vedic dharma and themselves Vaidikas. Since the first millennium, worship of Lord Vishnu has been known as Vaishnava path (*mārg*) and its followers are known as Vaishnavas; the worship of the goddess – Shakti – as the Shakta path and its followers as Shaktas, and so on. Today, some Hindus prefer the term *sanātan dharma* meaning "eternal (cosmic) order" not only because it is an indigenous term, but also because it highlights the significance of "*dharma*" – a core concept with moral implications that is shared by religious traditions that originated in ancient India – Hinduism, Buddhism, and Jainism.

The diversity in views with regard to Hinduism are not limited to its name. The tradition has been studied from a variety of perspectives since the nineteenth century. The categories used in a number of studies have historically been embedded in monotheistic perspectives with which Hinduism does not fully align. A bulk of early scholarship by European scholars in the nineteenth century was dedicated to the study of ancient sacred texts in Sanskrit. Early Indian scholars writing in English followed them. While these studies offered a window into worldviews of and debates among elite groups of ancient India, the relevance of the texts to the lives of Hindus historically and in contemporary times received little attention. Further, as a result of the focus on ancient texts, only the thought and concerns of their custodians, the priestly elite (called "Brahmins"), came to the fore as the essence of Hinduism. This led to a general impression that those who did not have access to Sanskrit texts did not have religious agency in the Hindu world. In the process, texts and practices important for a large number of Hindus, like the oral narrative about the goddess in Manju's village and Rukma's *rangolī*, were left out.

Since the later part of the twentieth century, regional sources like the songs of saint-poets sung by the Warkaris and practices related to local deities have been given considerable attention. Importantly, some practices of the marginalized groups, especially women and lower castes, have been brought to attention. Further, social and political processes related to caste hierarchies and religious nationalism have also been extensively studied. In addition to specialized studies, some excellent general introductions are also available. And yet, how diverse elite and non-elite facets of Hinduism relate to one another in the everyday lives of people can use greater consideration. In the absence of a single figure, doctrine, or text shared by all Hindus, the links that synthesize a priest's elaborate ritual worship of Lord Krishna's image in a magnificent temple with the dance of Chaitrali's students in a low caste neighborhood; or abstract designs representing the cosmos discussed in elite texts with Rukma's *rangolī* need more extensive exploration.

THE PLAN OF THE BOOK

This book offers an accessible introduction to Hinduism with an overview of diverse sources and practices embraced by Hindu individuals and groups, paying attention to how they relate to one another in creating a religious ethos that has endured for millennia. All currents of Hinduism are, of course, impossible to cover in a short introduction such as this. What the book aims to offer is a portrayal of the tradition in a critical but sensitive manner that helps readers understand worldviews, practices, and approaches to important matters in individual and social life broadly embraced by Hindus. In doing so, it keeps a major focus on popular practices and vernacular functional texts with which a large percentage of Hindu women and men from all layers of the Hindu society engage. This necessitates making only brief references of some sophisticated but exclusive elite texts and practices. The book presents the basics of Hinduism in three ways. First, it provides an overview of important written and oral sources for the beliefs and practices of Hindus. In this area, it discusses both elite Sanskrit and vernacular oral sacred texts that are used as primary religious sources by a large number of Hindus. Second, it surveys widely prevalent Hindu values, spiritual aspirations, and practices, many of which also take regionally specific forms. In discussing these, the book examines aspects of Hindu social structure that have been harshly discriminatory to some communities. But it also highlights regional popular practices that allow agency to them. It discusses in some detail practices of women including cooking and gifting certain foods on auspicious days. These non-elite practices, the book shows, relate in complex ways to elite texts and practices, sometimes in confirmation and sometimes in a subversive manner. Thirdly, it discusses distinctive features of Hinduism such as multiple voices heard in sacred texts, a host of deities, diverse modes of engaging with them and manifold paths to spiritual goals. Through the exploration of these basics, the book also aims to lead the reader to look closely at the relationship between culture and religion.

In the seven chapters that follow we will look at various facets of Hinduism in some detail. The first chapter briefly outlines major phases of the evolution of the network of Hindu traditions interweaving different currents in different contexts. It also touches upon the geographical spread of Hinduism tied to its recognition as a "world religion." The second and third chapters give an overview of important sacred texts in Sanskrit and oral vernacular texts with selected examples, many of which are narratives and poetry. These chapters explore widely accepted religious concepts, mythology of some pan-Hindu deities, and narratives glorifying local deities found in written and oral texts. A major focus of these chapters is to highlight the relationship between elite Sanskrit and popular vernacular texts through exchange, reinterpretation, resistance, and subversion. They stress that the flow of ideas, narratives, and tropes has not been in one direction – from elite to popular – but reciprocal. Each section discusses the historical context of the composition of specific texts, their significance at the time, and their contemporary relevance for Hindus. Familiarity with major texts in the two categories makes the discussion of the hierarchical organization of the society into castes in the next chapter accessible for the reader. The fourth chapter first discusses social organization of caste, and the discrimination faced by lower-caste communities within it. It then considers roles and status of Hindu women. The chapter also examines injunctions for an individual's moral duties as found in various texts – specific roles for men and women in different social groups, and general ideals for various stages of life – all embedded in the notion of *dharma*. The first four chapters make references to interactions with Buddhist and Jain religious traditions in ancient India as well as Islam in the medieval and early modern periods that have contributed to the evolution of the Hindu ethos.

The next three chapters focus specifically on people and their activities. Chapter 5 discusses religious activities of authoritative religious specialists such as priests, ascetics, and spiritual teachers as well as diverse lay groups. These activities include temple and home shrine worship rituals (*pūjā*), life cycle and other ceremonies performed by priests, meditation, ethically motivated actions, pilgrimage, festival celebrations, popular practices specific to regions or communities, sacred art performances, and women's roles in religious activities. The chapter will call attention to links among apparently disparate practices that are vital to the functioning of the Hindu world. Chapter 6 focuses on a major turning point in the history of Hinduism through its encounters with European groups that entered India and other parts of South-East Asia as merchants, missionaries, and colonizers in the wake of modernity. The chapter focuses on how these encounters vigorously stirred the Hindu ethos and led to paradoxical responses from various groups that continue to have impact in social and political spheres in India and elsewhere. The chapter also devotes a section to brief biographical sketches of three modern Hindu leaders. The final chapter focuses on Hinduism beyond Indian shores. It focuses on three major waves since the early first millennium that took Hindu texts and practices far beyond the boundaries of India – to Nepal and South-East Asia in the first millennium, to European countries and their colonies through migrations of Hindus in the nineteenth and the twentieth centuries, and acceptance of Hinduism by people of non-Hindu backgrounds in various countries around the world mainly through the influence of spiritual gurus. After the consideration of important aspects of Hinduism in seven chapters, the short epilogue turns to reflection on the nature of Hinduism as a religious tradition. It revisits the issue of definition of a religious ethos as an "-ism" and encourages the reader to distill for themselves the basics of Hinduism.

Each chapter contains one or more boxes explaining important terms and points. Visual context for discussion, provided by the figures here, can be amply enhanced by visiting the internet sites and watching videos for which links are provided in the bibliography where further reading suggestions for each chapter are provided. The works for which references are made in the text but which are not included in the short lists for exploration at the ends of chapters are included in the bibliography at the end of the book.

Table 0.1 Hinduism as a World Religion

Hinduism	A widely accepted term since the nineteenth century to denote a network of diverse religious traditions prevalent in India. The followers of the traditions used different terms earlier
Hindu population in the world	Third largest religious group in the world. Majority in India, Nepal, Mauritius, Bali (Indonesia); recognizable minority in Europe, the Americas and Middle-eastern countries
Origins	No single founder or text. The earliest texts are viewed as revealed texts by Hindus
Defining belief/ practice	Difficult to pinpoint. An immensely diverse tradition largely held together by a recognition of diversity in religious life as valid and some widely accepted values and spiritual goals

FURTHER EXPLORATION SUGGESTIONS

Hinduism Today, edited by Paramacharya Sadasivanathaswami. Kapaa, HI: Himalayan Academy. Accessed August 14, 2022. https://www. hinduismtoday.com/.

Lipner, Julius. 2010. *Hindus: Their Religious Beliefs and Practices*, 2nd ed. The Library of Religious Beliefs and Practices. Abingdon: Routledge.

Llewellyn, J. E. 2018. *Defining Hinduism: A Reader.* Abingdon: Routledge.

Mittal, Sushil, and Gene R. Thursby. 2008. *Studying Hinduism: Key Concepts and Methods.* London: Routledge.

Narayanan, Vasudha. "Diglossic Hinduism: Liberation and Lentils." *Journal of the American Academy of Religion* 68, no. 4 (2000): 761–779. http://www. jstor.org/stable/1465856.

Public Broadcasting Services. 2020. "Exploring Hinduism." Detroit: One Detroit. Video. https://www.pbs.org/video/exploring-hinduism-zjzodk/.

Radhakrishnan, S. 1927. *The Hindu View of Life: Upton Lectures Delivered at Manchester College, Oxford, 1926.* London: G. Allen & Unwin, Ltd.

Tharoor, Sashi. 2018. *Why I Am a Hindu.* New Delhi: Aleph.

1

HINDUISM IN HISTORY

As we have seen in the Introduction, the Hindu tradition, like its namesake river Sindhu, has been gathering numerous currents into an enormous flow over millennia. We did not discuss its origin since it is not possible to trace a single source or figure for it. In complete contrast to several other religious traditions that began with a single founder and gradually branched out in denominations, Hinduism comes together as a tradition from convergence of diverse currents. Therefore, it is helpful to look at historical phases and processes through which it slowly developed into its present form. We should, however, first briefly consider the geography of the Indian subcontinent that grounded this development. This subcontinent is the peninsular region in southern Asia that has the world's tallest mountains – the Himalayas – in the north, the Hindu Kush mountains in the northwest, the Arabian sea in the west, the bay of Bengal in the east, and the Indian ocean in the south. It has diverse landscapes with deserts, forests, large rivers, and fertile basins. As we will see in the course of the book, gradually, through hymns and narratives, the mountains, rivers, lakes, and seashores of the subcontinent became deeply inscribed in the imagination of Hindus as components of a living sacred landscape. This integral connection to the land contributes to Hinduism's

DOI: 10.4324/9781315303352-2

ethno-geographical dimensions. Yet, the subcontinent does not belong only to Hindus. The passes in the Hindu Kush that allow entry into it, the Himalayan ranges in which many cultures coexist, and the sea routes that bring traders have also contributed to the development of an immensely diverse religious ethos here. It is the birthplace of several world religions – Hinduism, Buddhism, Jainism, and Sikhism; has sizable populations following Islam and Christianity; and has also long been home to small Zoroastrian and Jewish communities. Conversely, Hinduism has been prevalent in diverse geographical contexts for centuries. While South Asia is the land of origin of Hinduism, since the mid first millennium, Hindu presence is found in south-east Asia; and from the late second millennium in Africa, the middle east, Europe, and the Americas through migration or embracing of the tradition by local populations. Because of changing national boundaries, the maps of South Asia and of the world population of Hindus are not included in this book. But links to websites with maps are given in the suggestions for further exploration sections in appropriate chapters or in parenthesis within them.

In what follows we will consider how important sociopolitical contexts, migrations, composition of texts, encounters with other religious traditions, and reinterpretations of thought and practices have shaped the Hindu tradition through the millennia. This will help us see the tradition as evolving through phases rather than having an unalterably fixed "essence." The box at the end of each section lists enduring contributions of that phase, allowing us to develop an informed perspective on the current discourses and dispel some misconceptions.

PREHISTORY: INDUS VALLEY CIVILIZATION

The earliest phase of (pre)history of ancient India (of which north-western parts are now in Pakistan) known to us today was an urban civilization that was at its peak from ca 2600 BCE through 1700 BCE. It flourished in the basin of the river Indus and another river – the Saraswati – that ran parallel to it but later dried up. Artifacts and remains of its cities were first discovered in the nineteenth century and then through excavation in the early twentieth century.

They have since been extensively studied. Recent research indicates that it had been evolving for millennia from early food production phases and was spread in the Indian subcontinent much beyond the Indus basin. It was indeed the most expansive riverside civilization in the ancient world. All information about this civilization comes through archeological evidence since no text from it is available and the script seen on the excavated seals and signs has not been deciphered. The Indus Valley civilization, also known as the Harappan civilization (named after its city Harappa), had impressive city planning that included citadels, public baths, reservoirs, irrigation channels, precisely gridded streets as well as drainage and sewer systems. Its merchants traded in consumer goods with major centers of the known world of the time including China, Mesopotamia, Egypt, and the near East where it was possibly called "Meluha."

We know little about the social and religious life of the Indus Valley people in a definitive manner. But scholars offer some observations. The cities in this civilization had layered and diverse governing systems. They appear not to have had much warfare. In the area of religious life, public structures like large bathing places may have served ritual functions. The most striking artifacts found at Harappan sites that quite likely had religious significance are small steatite seals with etched pictorial representations and inscriptions, possibly used for marking goods. Some motifs found in these etchings are as follows: a meditating male figure sometimes surrounded by animals – elephants, bulls, and mythical composite animals such as unicorn, vegetation, and female figures. A seal depicting an elaborate ritual scene for a deity is also found. Additionally, numerous clay female figurines found here are thought to have religious significance. The Indus Valley people likely worshipped many deities. While historical connections between later Hindu traditions and the Indus Valley civilization are not established, some elements from it – meditating male figures, female figurines of various types, inclusion of animals (especially elephants) and vegetation in religious iconography, and bathing places – bear resemblance to components in Indic religious traditions including Hinduism, Buddhism, Jainism, and Sikhism even today.

The cities of the Indus valley civilization disappeared around 1700 BCE. But it is thought plausible that elements of that civilization survived in rural interiors and were integrated into later religious ethos. In that case, the Indus Valley civilization can be considered the earliest phase to have offered a few elements to several religious traditions originating in the subcontinent including Hinduism. Another way in which the Indus Valley civilization has remained important in recent times is through debates about its inhabitants and the cause of its disappearance that often take political coloring. An earlier theory proposed that the civilization and its people were destroyed by invading Aryans from central Asia. This theory has been generally disregarded for the lack of evidence of warfare. The disappearance of the Indus civilization is now attributed to natural phenomena. There is also broad scholarly consensus that Aryans came to India as migrants and not invaders. But some schools of thought propose that the Aryans, who built the foundation of Hinduism with texts called "the Vedas," were, in fact, the inhabitants of the Indus Valley. This theory implies a continuum between Indus Valley civilization and Hinduism and gives Hindus the status of the original inhabitants of the subcontinent. This has remained a matter of bitter debates in academic and political spheres. In any case, the question of the occupants of the Harappan civilization has remained a riddle in the absence of textual evidence, which is found in abundance in all subsequent historical periods.

Indus Valley Civilization – Aspects of Interest in Contemporary Times

- seals with meditating male figures, animals such as elephants and vegetation
- female figurines
- public baths
- mystery about inhabitants

THE FOUNDATIONAL VEDIC CULTURE

Until the discovery of the Indus Valley civilization, the earliest known phase of Indian history was a culture that developed in its north-western regions in the early second millennium BCE and spread in the plains in the north and to south India over the subsequent centuries. It was the foundational phase of Hinduism. In contrast to the Indus Valley civilization, innumerable texts from this phase are available. The people who composed the texts identified themselves as *ārya* ("noble," "Aryan" in English). Scholars generally agree that the Aryans were pastoral groups from central Asia that migrated to India in waves through the Hindu Kush mountain passes starting in the early second millennium BCE. They brought with them hymns in the archaic Sanskrit language and religious practices that closely paralleled texts and practices of groups in ancient Persia (Iran) who are also believed to have migrated there from the same general region in central Asia. Archaic Sanskrit was an Indo-European language from which classical Sanskrit and other Indo-Aryan languages developed later.

The earliest extant text of the Aryans is a collection of hymns called "the *Rig Veda*," the first of the four Vedas and one of the oldest extant religious texts in the world, dated around 1500 BCE. Like core sacred texts in other world religions, the hymns of the *Rig Veda* (RV now on) were collected and systematically classified into chapters in a period later than their composition. It is possible that several popular hymns in circulation before this compilation were left out and are now lost forever. The next three Vedas, *Sāma*, *Yajur*, and *Atharva* (SV, YV, and AV now on), were composed in the next few centuries and draw heavily from RV. All Vedas have several parts. In addition to the main texts called the *saṃhitās*, many ancillary texts were developed for each Veda. The latter provide exegesis on texts, explanation for Vedic rituals, or mystical reflection on them. Together, these texts form the Vedic corpus. The term "Veda" is derived from a word that means "to know" and is a cognate of English "wit." A large number of Hindus consider the Vedas the most authoritative, inspired, and timeless repository of knowledge originally heard by ancient sages – *śruti*. The Vedic literature offers a wealth of information about the progression of the Aryan culture in north India for a millennium beginning in the second half of the second millennium BCE. It is important to keep in view, however, that these texts provide only the elite Aryan perspective on the early cultural and religious developments in that context. Texts reflecting perspectives and contributions of the diverse non-Aryan inhabitants of the land with whom Aryans interacted in a variety of ways – conflict, exchange, collaboration – are not available. Their contributions can only be inferred from the Vedic corpus.

The Vedic era can be broadly divided into two phases – (a) early Vedic (1300–1000 BCE), starting with RV, and (b) later Vedic, after the completion of the four *saṃhitā*s. Several hymns of RV refer to rivers of north-western India and Afghanistan indicating that the early Vedic culture flourished in that region. The hymns, addressing a host of divinities associated with natural elements such as rivers, fire, water, and rains suggest that they were sung in pastoral clans slowly evolving into agrarian communities. The social milieu was not complex. It did not have an elaborate political system, but simple rural communities organized in close-knit clans/tribes. The clans/tribes competed for cattle and pastures among themselves and with non-Aryan groups referred to as *dasyu*s and *dāsa*. Since the term *dāsa* came to mean "servant" in the later classical Sanskrit, the term has been sometimes seen in modern discourses as indicating subordination of the original inhabitants of the land by the Aryans. However, historian Romila Thapar suggests that during the early Vedic period, the terms *ārya* and *dāsa* likely indicated linguistic/cultural identities only. Similarly, a hymn in the last chapter of RV (10.90, considered a later composition) is viewed as indicating the beginning of the caste system – organization of the Hindu society with hereditary hierarchies. The hymn says that when the Supreme being sacrificed himself, from the mouth arose priests (Brahmins), from the arms warriors (Kshatriyas), from thighs craftsmen/traders (Vaishyas), and from the feet servants (Shudras). The hymn is viewed as establishing social hierarchy. Sanskrit scholars and translators of RV Stephanie Jamison and Joel Brereton, however, maintain that this was a social model and not a social reality during the Vedic period. There is also no indication in the hymn that the division of the society was meant to be hereditary. The idea of hierarchy is present here in embryonic form.

As concerns gender relations, the social context as reflected in RV was patriarchal. But the text does contain several references to female figures – divine, semi-divine, and human – and includes their voices. Women, who generally appear in wifely roles, are confident of their sexuality and at least in one case is able to remind her husband of his duties according to *dharma*. One woman, Ghosha, is mentioned as a contributor to RV (10.39–10.40). Jamison and Brereton indicate that because of a specific ritual focus of RV, the text gives little information on religious life outside of it. Since the RV hymns were compiled in a single text at a later date by elite men, there is a possibility (however remote) that some hymns composed by women were lost. As with most social dimensions, the issue of the position of women in the RV period remains a matter of public debate, with some arguing that they had liberated status and others that they were subordinated. The reality was likely somewhere in between.

With regard to religious ideology, early Vedic people were generally not concerned with the afterlife, but rather with life here and now. RV hymns mention ancestors, but mainly as the ones who provided models for sacrifice (1.42.5, 1.62.2, etc.). There are very few mentions of afterlife in RV and only one to *svarga* (heaven 10.95). The concept of cycles of birth was not prevalent yet. The Vedic people prayed to their deities representing various natural elements – fire, winds, rains, waters, rivers, the sun, the moon, dawn – often in a tender affectionate voice and asked for health, material prosperity, well-being of their clans, progeny (mostly sons), and victory in skirmishes. Religious life generally centered around the family, indicating the significance of a householder in the society. However, there is also a passing reference to ascetics in a hymn. A core religious practice was singing Vedic hymns while making offerings (generally of a drink named *soma*) to all deities through the deity of fire – Agni. The deities, in return, were believed to provide their worshippers good crops and happy life. Through such exchange, it was thought, humans and deities contributed to the maintenance of cosmic order called *ṛta*. The Vedic pantheon of deities was almost like a corporation with each of its members having a specific portfolio. The hymns to these diverse deities were compositions of several sages. Thus, a multilayered pantheon and multivocality were salient features of this religious culture, eliminating the possibility of absolute power and authority for a single figure.

Over the centuries, as the Vedic culture moved eastward to the Gangetic plains from northwest India, its social organization, religious ideology, and the nature of practices began to change. The small clan structure gave way to a more complex society and advanced political system. A hierarchical society divided into four groups mentioned in the Vedic hymn mentioned earlier – priests, warriors, merchants/traders, and servants – was now becoming a reality. Elaborate sacrifices performed at temporary fire altars began to be officiated by special classes of priests. While such grand sacrifices, often performed for communal good, were generally sponsored by the king or the wealthy, simpler household rituals for common people also developed. Both types of rituals were performed by couples reaffirming the centrality of householder life. Gradually, sacrificial rituals came to be seen as having greater power to offer desired results than even the deities. They were viewed almost like today's technical operations requiring precise performance. Priests with knowledge of these rituals emerged as the highest class in the society. With increased complexity in rituals and political life, the priests and the warriors began to enjoy great status and influence. They dominated over others, especially servants who often came from non-Aryan communities. A stratified social system was taking shape. At the same time, the widely spreading Vedic Aryan culture was also integrating elements from other cultures it encountered.

The later Vedic culture phase also saw close interactions with pre-existent *śramana* (ascetic) traditions and the rise of internal debates. The ascetic ideal found in passing in RV expanded. A new current of philosophical thought was introduced by thinkers who began to reinterpret ritual sacrifice in terms of interior spiritual quest. Many lived in forests, practiced meditation, and had disciples with whom they engaged in spiritual dialogs recorded in Vedic texts called "Upanishads." Here, voices of a few learned women are also heard. One of them is a major debater, indicating a degree of right to education for women. The texts also point to the significance of a spiritual teacher (guru), which has remained important in Hinduism till this date. While the Upanishads were composed in diverse schools, several share the concept of an underlying reality of all existence called "Brahman." This implied that an individual self – *ātman* – was in essence identical with it. By the time of composition of important Upanishads, the notion that a soul transmigrates through cycles of rebirth in this world (*saṃsāra*) was widespread in India. It also became a part of the Vedic ethos. The spiritual striving for an individual in the Upanishadic schools consisted in gaining liberation from *saṃsāra* and realizing one's identity with Brahman. While the Vedic culture was thus being stirred internally, a number of *śramaṇa* traditions and materialist schools of thought challenged the authority of the Vedas and Vedic rituals. Two of these, Buddhism and Jainism, which shared with the Vedic schools a belief in transmigration, eventually emerged as independent religions.

The religious practices prevalent in the Vedic period changed in later Hinduism. But many aspects of the Vedic culture continue to remain important till today.

Enduring Aspects of the Vedic Religion

Ideological

- a focus on sanctifying all aspects of life by drawing on cosmic energies
- recognition of debates and diverse religious perspectives as valid
- focus on family life, with stress on responsibility to others and the world
- belief in rebirth and spiritual striving for liberation from it
- identity of the soul with the Ultimate reality (Brahman)
- reverence toward natural elements and belief in a kind of corporation of divine beings rather than in one almighty God

Religious Practices

- chanting of mantras
- meditation
- having fire as the divine witness in life cycle and other rituals

Social Organization

- early development of hierarchical social organization (caste), from which the Hindu society is still struggling to fully break free

FORMATIVE PHASE – CLASSICAL HINDUISM

If the Vedic era can be viewed as the foundational phase of Hinduism, the next historical phase, beginning with the last centuries before the common era and extending into the early centuries of the second millennium CE, can be considered its most formative period. In this phase, often called the period of classical Hinduism, a number of its core components that are prevalent today developed. Politically, north India saw significant turns during this phase. Alexander the Great knocked India's doors at its north-west with one victory in 326 BCE; but then left. The following centuries saw invasions on the north-west of India by rulers from central Asia – Bactrians, Kushans, Sakas. And they also saw the rise of successive powerful royal dynasties in various parts of the subcontinent – Maurya, Shunga, Gupta, Gurjara-Pratihara, Cholas, Palas, Rashtrakutas – whose reign brought stability and prosperity in their territories. Each emperor was more favorable to a specific school of religious thought, often for political reasons. But most of them supported diverse religious groups within their territories. Hindu traditions prospered under the rule of many of these.

During the last centuries before the Common Era and the early centuries into it, the Vedic religious culture faced major challenges, especially from the popularity of Buddhist and Jain traditions and patronage to them by royal courts and wealthy merchants. The mighty Emperor Ashoka of the Maurya dynasty, for example, greatly supported Buddhism and even sent emissaries to Sri Lanka to propagate it. The Vedic tradition experienced a setback. The response of the adherents of the Vedic tradition – the Vaidikas – to this challenge was complex, multifaceted, and often paradoxical. On the one hand, many texts composed by the priestly class of Brahmins in this phase elaborated on moral duties (*dharma*) of individuals and hereditary obligations of various castes, which were hierarchically organized with a notion of inherent purity and pollution. Some injunctions contained in these texts were extremely harsh for castes identified as so impure that they were rendered "untouchable." Norms that made women completely dependent on men were also established. Some of these have remained influential through the centuries.

On the other hand, the tradition showed immense flexibility in incorporating elements from non-Vedic regional cultures, which eventually allowed it to reemerge as predominant in India. Several non-Vedic deities became identified with minor divinities appearing in the Vedas and began to be worshipped widely. Other regional deities were integrated into the Hindu pantheon through extensive religious narratives, which have remained at the core of Hindu life. The deities who emerged as the most prominent were Shiva, Vishnu, and the great Goddess. Each had multiple manifestations or incarnations and associated divine beings as family or assistants. Days associated with the deities as per their narratives began to mark yearly calendars as festivals; and places mentioned in their narratives began to get woven into large pilgrimage networks. Regional communities and even non-Indian immigrants and tribes became incorporated in the caste organization at different levels. These exchanges between the Vedic and non-Vedic cultures were deeply transformative for the Hindu tradition.

As centuries passed, large brick and stone temples to various deities with installation of anthropomorphic or aniconic images were built with royal or community patronage. Systematic ritual worship of images performed by priests became as central to Hinduism as Vedic sacrifices once were, but with a significant difference. Unlike the temporary altars around which only priests performed sacrifices, construction of temples with complex ritual cycles also engaged architects, masons, sculptors, gardeners, cooks, dancers, and musicians who came from different professional guilds. While the roles were organized in a strict ritual hierarchy with the priest still being in charge of the core ceremonies, they allowed entry points with religious agency for many others. Further, several regional practices outside of priestly domains, such as votive rites involving worship of specific trees or groves, also found religious validity. The coexistence of ritual hierarchy and validation of religious agency of people from all layers of the society in informal contexts infused the emerging ethos of Hinduism with vitality. The new ethos had all the important components of Hinduism as we know it today.

In the transformation of the Vedic tradition into classical Hinduism, varied genres of religious and secular texts in classical

Sanskrit written during this phase played a major role. As seen earlier, many priestly texts focused on *dharma* or normative moral, ethical, and social code (but not exactly "command-ment" or "law") and have been greatly influential. Yet these are not the texts that average Hindus read or of which they know even the titles. It is another class of texts emerging from this period that have since been central to religious life in all layers of the Hindu society and to the tradition's transmission from one generation to another in a myriad of ways. These are narra-tive texts in classical Sanskrit including two epics – the *Ramayana* and the *Mahabharata* – with numerous subplots and the Puranas containing extensive mythology of various divinities. In the narrative literature, social norms prescribed in *dharma* texts are sometimes reinforced, sometimes subverted, and sometimes challenged, giving an indication that there was consistent ques-tioning of those norms within the expanding Hindu culture. Perhaps this was because the narratives drew heavily from pre-existing non-Vedic, non-Sanskrit sources which did not align with the prescriptions of the *dharma* texts. The resultant tension between the elite prescriptions and their internal ques-tioning has been an integral and richly creative part of the Hindu tradition. It is a significant basic of Hinduism that often gets overlooked in discourses about it.

Stories from the epics, two of the longest in the world, have been retold and reinterpreted innumerable times in Indic and other lan-guages as well as in their Buddhist and Jain versions. The same is the case with mythologies. The narratives portray interactions among divine and human characters in ways that appeal to human emotions. Their popularity contributed to the changing religious ethos in two important ways. First, it promoted personal devotion (*bhakti*) to a deity as a vital religious path open to all. By the early centuries of the first millennium, along with action or *karma* (ritual or otherwise) and spiritual knowledge or *jñāna*, *bhakti* was established as a valid reli-gious pursuit in Hinduism. In the latter half of the first millennium, it emerged with a new vitality with a regional religio-cultural devel-opment in the Tamil region of South India where popular devotional lyrics/songs in the local language dedicated to Shiva by one group of poets and to Vishnu by another became the basis of two regional sects. With these songs, which were sung widely by people, began a historical trend of vernacularization through which *bhakti* filtered through layers of the Hindu society. Second, the narratives, which are always open to reinterpretation, provided the basis for literary, visual, and performative arts that have thrived for centuries not only in India but also outside of it in the Himalayan regions and south-east Asia where Hindu influences traveled. For example, the famous carvings in ancient Angkor Wat temples in Cambodia, shadow puppet shows still prevalent in Indonesia, and dance dramas in Bali testify to the enduring popularity of the narratives.

In addition to the narratives, several texts were composed by various thinkers who accepted the authority of the Vedas and belonged to six schools of philosophy or perspectives (*darśana*) – Nyāya, Vaiśesśika, Sāṃkhya, Mimāṃsā, Yoga, and Vedānta. These schools focused on logic, nature and components of reality, meaning of rituals, and disciplines for self-realization. While these schools were not necessarily theologically oriented, their insights helped create an overlap among theologies of various deities in diverse sects emerging in different periods. Along with religious texts, secular poetic and dramatic literature as well as treatises on subjects such as health, aesthetics, performing arts, lovemaking, astronomy, and astrology also alluded recurrently to the sacred narratives, contributing to their growing popularity and offering cultural padding in the emerging religious ethos.

Enduring Aspects, Classical Hinduism Phase

Ideological

- stress on one's moral duty to family and society according to social position
- three religious paths – karma, *jnān*, and *bhakti*
- context-sensitive *dharma*
- reinforcing, debate and subversion of dharmic norms in narrative texts – continuation of multiple perspectives

Social

- stratification of caste hierarchies
- restrictions on women
- interactions with non-Aryans; incorporation of their deities and practices

Worship Practices (Mainly Based on Sacred Narratives)

- temples to Puranic and regional deities
- ritual worship (*pūjā*) of divine images in grand and small temples
- various types of offerings to the images by priestly and non-priestly temple associates
- singing of hymns, dance
- retelling of narratives in oral and artistic forms
- pilgrimage to sites associated with narratives

MEDIEVAL AND EARLY MODERN PHASE

The medieval and the early modern periods here mean the period from the late tenth through the eighteenth centuries. It was another phase of major political shifts and their enduring impact on the religious ethos of South Asia. The second millennium was marked by two major developments in Hinduism. One was the extensive spread of vernacular devotional traditions, composition of treatises on various arts and commentaries on Sanskrit texts, and temple-building activities. And the other, its close interactions with two monotheistic traditions – first Islam and then Christianity – as well as cultures of people who brought those to India.

During the late centuries of the first millennium, powerful dynasties ruled over large parts of India. Islam had been introduced into the subcontinent through trade. From early centuries of the second millennium arrived Muslim missionaries (*dāis*) as well as mystics called Sufis who contributed greatly to the spread of Islam in India. Invaders from central Asia also frequented India. The early invaders did not settle here. But when the later invaders began to settle in north India and extended their reign over large territories, the extensive encounter between the religious ethos of the subcontinent and Islam was complex. At times, it entailed bitter conflicts and subjugation of the defeated side; but in many ways it was also an encounter of fruitful mutual exchange that led to the creation of a rich composite culture.

One of the most important developments within the Hindu traditions during this period was development of *bhakti* literature in regional languages of north India, especially devotional lyrics composed by saintly poets dedicated to various Hindu deities as well as the formless Ultimate (whom they generally called Rām and only sometimes Brahman). Traditions of *bhakti* embedded in songs of saint-poets had already emerged in the Tamil speaking region. In north India, the replacement of Sanskrit by Persian as the language of powerful courts had an impact on patronage patterns and coincided with the development of regional languages. Saint-poets contributed greatly to the early poetic traditions of various regional languages. Their songs of intense devotion circulated widely through community performances in all strata of the society in their regions. Some songs referred to and reinterpreted Puranic narratives; some contained teaching about inner search as in the Upanishads; many critiqued caste hierarchies. The saint-poets came from all strata of the society and often gathered disciples from various castes. Many popular saint-poets were women who challenged patriarchy. Legends about the lives of regional saint-poets became equally popular, often beyond their home regions. These songs and narratives have made regional *bhakti* traditions an enduring component of the Hindu religious ethos. The Warkaris we met in the Introduction, for example, sing songs of Marathi saint-poets of medieval Maharashtra. Parallel traditions of vernacular popular devotional songs also evolved in Islam and Sikhism, which developed during this period. All of them shared vocabulary and imagery, allowing circulation of several songs across religious boundaries. Their enduring popularity is evident in their continued performance in religious and secular cultural contexts even today.

Another important legacy of this era is the grand temples built in various parts of the country. While some large temples had been built by the end of the first millennium, many that continue to be visited as major pilgrimage sites were built during the second millennium with impressive development of regional architectural styles. Musical repertoires for various temple rituals were extensively developed by some sects during this time. In south India, composers/musicians like Purandardas (fifteenth century), Kanakdas (sixteenth century), and Tyagaraja (eighteenth century) made important contributions to devotional music. In north India, a classical music style with Persian elements added to the already well-developed Indian music was incorporated in temple music. Similarly, mythological paintings included in manuscripts in many parts of the subcontinent showed Persian influence during and after the reign of the Mughal emperors (sixteenth–eighteenth centuries) who were major patrons of that art. Despite some conflicts inevitable in encounters of completely different religious ideologies, the first six centuries of the second millennium was a period of growth of regional *bhakti* currents and sects in various parts of India that reached all layers of society. It was also a period of innovations in literary, visual, and performative religious art with enduring implications.

In the second half of the second millennium, Christians from European countries also began to arrive on the Indian shores. A small Christian community had lived in South India since the early centuries of the Common Era. With the coming of the Europeans as traders or missionaries to India, other Christian communities were established through conversions. Early missionary work in this phase was often based on dialog. But the trade networks gradually turned into imperial colonies. Colonization changed the nature of Hindu encounters with European Christianity in the modern era beginning in the late eighteenth century.

Enduring Aspects, Medieval, and Early Modern Phase

Ideological

- devotion (*bhakti*) to a single or multiple deities or to a formless divine as a major religious path
- multiplicity of voices from all classes of the society – women, Dalits – among regional saint-poets

Social

- **vernacularization of Hindu traditions**
- **disregard for social hierarchies in relation to the divine (but not as a social norm) in several *bhakti* communities**
- **interactions with followers of Islam, Sikhism, and Christianity**

Practices

- **singing of devotional songs of regional saint-poets and retelling narratives about them**
- **pilgrimage**
- **temple building**
- **patronage for temples, religious paintings, music, and dance**

MODERN AND POSTMODERN ERAS

The European colonizers introduced secular education, post-enlightenment thought, and some new ways of governance in India. Their intellectuals and administrative staff had diverse attitudes toward the native religions including Hinduism. Some admired and even romanticized the spiritual and intellectual achievements of Hindus. But many were scathingly critical of its multiple deities, popular practices like tree worship, and its social organization. Their portrayal of Hinduism was disparaging. Some of them represented Hindus as culturally backward to the degree of repulsion; but worthy of a chance to become civilized. Of the competing European groups, the British ultimately emerged as the winners and often justified their rule as a civilizing mission.

The responses of Hindu intellectuals and leaders to European representation of their tradition were equally diverse. Some were defensive; and some fiercely disputed the critique. Some highlighted philosophical concepts regarding the self as the core of Hinduism; some advocated reform; and some engaged revival of what they considered a "golden" past. These two responses are associated with several "reform" and "revival" movements beginning the nineteenth century. A major focus of several movements that arose in the nineteenth and early twentieth centuries were teachings of selected sacred texts – especially the Vedas, the Upanishads, and the *Bhagavad Gita*. Many religious leaders rejected image worship and caste distinctions. Some also collaborated with British officials to establish legal interventions for women's issues. Participation of women in public life saw remarkable increase. Some reforms in the Hindu society with support of the British were indeed helpful. Yet, the consistently negative representation of their tradition in European discourses also led many Hindus to fiercely defend it. They felt an urgent need to be champions of Hinduism when the administrative policies formally included religion as a marker of identity in the census. A few Hindu groups, like similar groups from other religious communities, began to articulate pride in their tradition in a polemical manner, contributing to growing religious tensions. India's independence with its partition into Hindu majority India and Muslim majority Pakistan as well as communal violence that followed it contributed to the continuation of religion-based frictions on both sides of the border, with severely damaging impact on the minorities.

There have been three other important developments since the nineteenth century. One is the emergence of large guru-centered communities. Even though saint-poets of the previous age also had communities of disciples around them, the scale of the new communities is unprecedented. The shifting focus from temple rituals to the study of philosophy and the rise of an educated middle-class have contributed to large communities of people gathering around spiritual mentors – both male and female – who come from diverse castes. Today, there are hundreds of guru communities of which class rather than caste forms the basis. The other development has been two waves of Hindu diasporas. The first wave occurred in the context of colonial rule when numerous Indians were taken as indentured laborers to European colonies such as Mauritius, Trinidad, Fiji, and British Guyana. Some merchants and professionals were also a part of this wave. These communities kept their tradition alive in difficult circumstances with meager means. Hindu diaspora also occurred after independence when Indian professionals and workers migrated to European countries and the Americas in the search of opportunities. As their number increased, they developed temples and Hindu community life in their new home-lands. A third noteworthy phenomenon of prevalence of Hinduism outside of India has been through individuals and communities embracing it, not through heritage but often as disciples of Hindu spiritual gurus. In all these non-Indian contexts, practice of Hinduism has adapted to its environment.

Modern Times (Multiple Responses to Modernity in the Colonial Contexts)

Ideological

- focus on philosophical texts and concepts such as Brahman (Ultimate Reality)
- rejection of image worship by some
- service to the downtrodden as a path

Social

- awareness of distinctive Hindu identity
- social reform and reassertion of Hindu ideals
- tensions and violent conflicts among religious communities
- women's education and participation in public life
- movements against caste discrimination
- diaspora of Hindus in waves
- non-Hindus embracing Hindu faith

Practices

- study of texts
- Yoga practices
- learning from spiritual gurus

As the above survey indicates, growing from its ancient roots, Hinduism has emerged as a multilayered tradition in both Indian and non-Indian contexts. Despite its tremendous diversity, some of its facets have remained widely (but not uniformly) prevalent. These are: a focus on sanctification of life in religious practices, acceptance of validity of diverse religious views and practices, stress on social responsibility, absence of centralized authority, and an understanding of the divine radically different from monotheistic traditions. In terms of social organization, the relevance of caste is diminishing but it still continues to factor in marriages and politics. People in the lowest castes formerly considered too polluted to touch— now known as Dalits – continue to struggle against discrimination. Women have made tremendous strides in education and professional life, but they are still striving for equality in all spheres. However, it should be noted that by and large, Hindu individuals and communities have welcomed change. They have generally supported the accommodations made in the Indian Constitution for the marginalized castes and tribes in education and government jobs (termed "reservation"), even though instances of anti-reservation protests have also been noted. Leaders from marginalized communities have striven to politically empower them. Some people are beginning to accept gender fluidity as well. A few organizations are focused on contributing to peace-building in the world, while there is simultaneously a rise of intense religious nationalism in some pockets. In the chapters that follow, we will look more closely at some aspects discussed above.

Table 1.1 Timeline

2600–1700 BCE	Indus Valley civilization at its peak
1500–500 BCE	Development and Spread of Vedic culture
	Rise of Buddhism and Jainism in India
322 BCE–650 CE	Powerful Empires – Maurya, Gupta, Pallava
200 BCE–1200 CE	Development of classical Hinduism; Hindu cultures and influences traveling to south-east Asian countries
1200–1800	Dynamic interactions with Islam and development of regional devotional traditions
1800–1947	Colonial experience, close encounter with European Christianity; Hindu diaspora in European colonies, early Hindu nationalism
1947–present	Partition of India and communal violence, diasporas in Europe and the Americas, Hindu identity in politics, Hindu gurus and development of Hindu communities worldwide. rise of Hindu nationalism

FURTHER EXPLORATION SUGGESTIONS

Basham, A. L. 1975. *A Cultural History of India.* Oxford: Clarendon Press.

Basham, A. L., and Kenneth G Zysk. 1989. *The Origins and Development of Classical Hinduism.* Boston, MA: Beacon Press.

Harappa. 1995–2022. "The Ancient Indian Valley Civilization 3500-1700 BCE." Accessed July 1, 2022. https://www.harappa.com/.

Hinduism Today. 2015. "History of Hindu India" Videos. Accessed July 1, 2022. https://www.youtube.com/playlist?list=PLkA3jcdbA5kR_NUZVYZIwKyStLiTXZYcu.

Klostermaier, Klaus K. 2014. *Hinduism: A Short History.* New York, NY: Oneworld Publications.

Michaels, Axel, and Barbara Harshav. 2004. *Hinduism: Past and Present.* Chapter 2. Princeton, NJ: Princeton University Press.

Wikimedia. N.d. Indian Subcontinent. Map. https://commons.wikimedia.org/wiki/File:Indian_subcontinent.JPG

2

FOUNDATIONAL AND FORMATIVE SACRED TEXTS AND CONCEPTS

In the Introduction we saw that the members of the Kulkarni family and their acquaintances, including Manju and the Warkari singers, draw on diverse sets of sacred texts – some in Sanskrit and some in their regional language Marathi. The term "scripture" in the sense of one singularly authoritative text, as understood in the "religions of the book," is not applicable in relation to Hinduism, which has a layered corpus of numerous sacred texts. However, the term "Hindu scriptures" is often used for the collection of ancient texts in Sanskrit that have historically (but not in the modern times) remained by and large in the custody of the priestly elite. These have certainly been regarded by a sizable percentage of Hindus as containing foundational spiritual principles of their faith. But if we want to look at the textual sources that are deeply integrated into the religious lives of average Hindus, along with these Sanskrit texts, we must also consider oral and written sacred texts in regional languages as authentic textual sources. The regional texts sometimes draw from, sometimes expand, and sometimes subvert the hallowed Sanskrit ones. Combined with the absence of a centralized ecclesial authority, the layered nature of sacred texts leads to distinctive dynamics of religious authority and agency in Hinduism. Priests, with their knowledge of authoritative texts,

2

DOI: 10.4324/9781315303352-3

have high status; but they are not in charge of regularly giving sermons based on scriptures in institutional settings as found in other religious contexts such as churches. People may read the texts on their own and may go to lectures by well-known interpreters, but not to priests. People's religious life to a large extent involves performing their preferred practices and engaging with selected Sanskrit or vernacular texts with or without a guiding figure.

In this chapter, we will get an overview of important texts in Sanskrit, considered the perfected divine language by many Hindus. As we noted in the Introduction, however, we will also keep in view that the contributions of ancient non-Aryan people and non-Sanskrit texts (oral or written) to Hinduism can be only glimpsed through the prism of Sanskrit texts. Because our focus is on the basics of Hinduism, texts significant exclusively for specific sects or those not of widespread usage will not be discussed. We will rather consider how various types of sacred texts are integrated in the religious lives of average Hindus. At the end of the first section simple pithy quotes are given in a box; for important concepts from texts discussed in other sections, the table at the end can be seen. In the next chapter, we will consider vernacular texts. A major focus of the chapters on texts is to highlight the relationship between Sanskrit and vernacular texts through exchange, expansion, reinterpretation, resistance, and subversion. They stress that the flow of ideas, narratives, and tropes has not been in one direction – from elite to popular – but reciprocal.

"REVEALED" TEXTS – *śruti*

As seen earlier, the Vedic corpus (ca 1500 BCE – the turn of the Common Era) forms the foundational textual resource for Hinduism. The corpus consists of main texts called *saṃhitā*s (collections of metrical or prose texts) and important ancillary texts – *brahmaṇa*s (explanations of rituals), *āraṇyaka*s (treatises composed by hermits explaining philosophical meanings of Vedic rituals), and Upanishads (dialogs of philosophical reflection) associated with each of the four Vedas – RV, SV, YV, and AV (*Rig, Sāma, Yajur*, and *Atharva* Vedas). As mentioned earlier, the approximate meaning of the term Veda is "knowledge." The Vedas are seen by most Hindus as the texts embodying eternal truth and containing principles of a harmonious cosmic order (*ṛta*) that were heard by ancient sages in inspired states. They are therefore called *śruti* and were transmitted orally for hundreds of years before being committed to writing, which was seen as inferior to the heard texts. Even today, traditional Veda schools use memorization and recitation as vital methods of transmission. As inspired texts, the Vedas are also considered *apauruṣeya* (not human) compositions. But they are not seen as "the words/message of God." This is an important "basic" of Hinduism. The references to the transcendent are often impersonal (as principle like *ṛta* or Brahman); and the host of deities are referred to as manifesting/representing or serving that transcendent. Another important point to keep in view is that even though Vedas are considered to be the most authoritative texts and have influenced several aspects of Hinduism, except for experts, Hindus neither study them in their entirety, nor refer to them in religious lives. The high regard is ceremonious to a great extent.

Vedic *saṃhitā*s (chiefly RV) contain three main types of hymns. A large number are dedicated to deities (several associated with natural elements or symbolizing cosmic energies) who support the maintenance of *ṛta* and give gifts to their worshippers. Several hymns are infused with a sense of wonder and use an affectionate tone. Chief among the deities is the martial deity Indra, praised for releasing life-giving rains held up by demon Vṛtra. Other major deities include the priest-like Agni (fire) who represents all deities at sacrificial rites and carries offerings to them, Soma (a plant and drink), and Varun (affiliated with waters and also the moral judge of people). Among the goddesses important are Prithvi (earth), Ushas (dawn), Aditi (mother of deities), and importantly, Vac (the goddess of speech). With a specific association for each deity, the pantheon was almost like a corporation. The hymns, however, suggest that martial skills as represented by Indra, and priestly knowledge as represented by Agni, were significant for the Vedic people and may be linked to the elevated status of warriors and priests in the society.

A few hymns in the RV also offer different theories about the Creation or simply ask questions about it. It was not problematic for the Vedic people to have diverse perspectives on creation including an agnostic one. A hymn dedicated to the "Golden Embryo"

(10.121) as the source of creation asks who the ultimate creator – One – is and calls that being Prajapati (the Lord of creatures). Another hymn (10.90) says that the creation came into being when the Supreme man with "thousand hands" and "thousand eyes," sacrificed himself. As mentioned in Chapter 1, the Hindu caste system is often traced to this hymn. The *Nāsadiya* hymn (10.129) goes to the extent of speculating whether there is any Creator. It ends with ambivalence about whether the lord of "the highest heaven" knows the truth about the creation or "maybe even he does not know."

The *saṃhitā*s also contain passages related to ethical, environmental, material, astronomical, and social themes – interrelated aspects of the cosmic order in the Vedic view. This view held that humans share the power of imagination and speech with divine beings and contribute significantly to the maintenance of this order through prayers, rites, and proper behavior. A few verses, including a mantra for *śanti* (peace) in the cosmos – in earth, water, air, and space – from the *saṃhitā*s, give some idea of that worldview. The RV verses are translated by Ralph Griffith (1896); the peace mantra is my translation.

> May he [Indra] stand by us in our need and in abundance for our wealth: May he come nigh us with his strength. (RV.1.5.3)
>
> Bounteous is he who gives unto the beggar who comes to him in want of food and feeble.
> Success attends him in the shout of battle.
> He makes a friend of him in future troubles.
>
> Let the rich satisfy the poor implorer and bend his eye upon a longer pathway.
> Riches come now to one, now to another, and like the wheels of cars are ever rolling. (RV.10.117.3, 5)
>
> May peace prevail in the sky!
> May peace prevail in ethereal space! May peace be on earth!
> May peace be in waters, in herbs, in vegetation!. May there always be peace alone!
>
> May all beings see me with the eyes of a friend!
> May I see all beings with the eyes of a friend!
> May we all look at each other with friends' eyes! (YV 36.17-18)

The *saṃhitā* texts were used for sacrificial rites during the Vedic period. Considered infallible in achieving their stated aims and recreating the cosmic order at the microcosmic level, Vedic prayers and fire sacrifices were performed around temporary altars structured with precise geometric formulas.

Among other categories of Vedic texts, the Upanishads (also called "Vedanta" or the last sections of the Vedas) are the most influential texts of Hindu metaphysical thought, generally in the form of dialogues between a teacher and his students who sit near him. Of a large number of Upanishads, 13 (and sometimes 10) are considered principal. These were composed between the seventh-century BCE and the early centuries of the Common Era. It was a time when the concept of endless rebirths of a person took deep roots in Indic religious thought. Liberation from this loop emerged as a cherished spiritual goal. Encounters with pre-existing non-Vedic *śramaṇa* traditions that stressed asceticism and meditation for the fulfillment of that goal deeply influenced Vedic thinkers. In many Upanishads, meditation is recognized as an effective path for knowledge and liberation. The orientation of the Upanishads is inward and mystical. In some, performance of sacrifice is interpreted as inner search. Several Upanishads speak of an eternal/ Ultimate spiritual reality – termed "Brahman" – underlying all existence (including deities), which has no gender or attributes. The individual self, called *ātman*, is in essence identical with Brahman. Realizing the identity of one's *ātman* with Brahman with the guidance of a teacher began to be seen as a liberating path by many. A few Upanishads integrate the element of devotion to a divine being, recognized as residing in all creatures.

Some Upanishads also dealt with the emerging social order of the time. The texts refer to two spheres of experience – the ever-changing phenomenal and the timeless spiritual. They deal with the latter and reject differences of caste or gender at that level. *Chāndogya*, generally dated before the rise of Buddhism and Jainism, for example, has a section where a servant woman's son with unknown patrimony – Satyakama – is recognized as a Brahmin (priest) because of his truthfulness (*Chāndogya* 4.1–5). Such passages indicate that differing interpretations of caste were prevalent at least in some contexts at the time.

The *śruti* texts laid the foundation of some important aspects of Hinduism as we know it today. First, they established the validity of multiplicity of voices and debates in the area of religious inquiry. Second, they developed two major impersonal principles – Brahman as the deepest essential reality of all existence and a cosmic order (*r̥ta*, later *dharma*) as its regulating principle – in Hindu thought. Third, the hierarchical and hereditary order of caste that Hindu society has long followed was seen at least in its embryonic form in them. Yet, they also offer a few models for giving primacy to moral qualities rather than hereditary caste, which has found a few adherents in each phase of the history of Hinduism. Fourth, the early delineations of the three religious paths – *karma* (action – ritual and moral), *bhakti* (devotion), and *jñāna* (knowledge) – that Hindus consider valid today can be seen in them. Fifth, in the area of rituals, Vedic mantras are still recited in temple worship and ceremonies; and Agni remains the divine witness at weddings and other life cycle ceremonies. Fifth, they shaped the Hindu view of nature as sacred, which is still prevalent and is considered significant for environment protection by many followers of the tradition. All these aspects are embedded in the view of the universe as a sacred harmonious entity. Humans can harness its power for enriching their lives; but must contribute to maintain it. For Rukma, whom we met in the introduction, inviting the sacred powers to her home with auspicious designs and watering the basil plant are integral to religious life.

"REMEMBERED" TEXTS – *smr̥ti*

If the *śruti* texts are foundational texts of Hinduism, several texts that fall in the category of *smr̥ti* (literally "remembered") can be called its formative corpus. These texts in diverse genres are considered lower in authority only to *śruti* since they are not seen as "revealed" but as authored by great sages. The category of *smr̥ti* is somewhat fluid and different texts may be included in it in various contexts. But broadly, they include treatises and narratives that recognize the authority of the Vedas and purport to enhance their understanding. This is significant because a bulk of the *smr̥ti* literature was written during a few centuries before and after the turn of the Common Era when several schools of religious thought were challenging the authority of the Vedas. These schools, including Buddhism and Jainism, were characterized as *nāstika* – "[believing] it [Brahman] does not exist." The *smṛti* texts were seen as belonging to *āstika* ("believing") schools. They served the dual functions of responding to the *nāstika* schools and offering relevant interpretations of the Vedic thought and practices in the new contexts. They offer vital examples of adaptability for which Hinduism is known.

The early *smṛti* corpus developed with six auxiliary branches of Vedic knowledge (called *vedāngas*) – phonetics, grammar, prosody, ritual, astronomy/astrology, and etymology – that contributed significantly to later theories and practice of music (*gāndhrava*) and architecture (*sthāpatya*), life sciences (*āyurveda*), and Hindu schools of philosophy. An important section of these is formed by *śrauta sūtras* and *gṛhya sūtras*, texts related to sacrificial and domestic (especially rites of passage) rituals, respectively. Of these, the latter are still widely prevalent in ceremonies such as name giving and weddings. Another set of the *smṛti* texts that have been greatly influential are: (a) treatises on social order and appropriate pursuits in individual life and (b) sacred narratives. The texts in the former group are focused on prescribing *dharma* (moral codes); the ones in the latter are formed by two epics and mythologies in texts called the Puranas ("related to ancient times"). The texts focused on *dharma* prescribe norms of ethical behavior and social obligations according to one's community of birth and stage in life. They have been vitally influential for Hindu social organization. But most Hindus know neither the titles of these texts nor their actual content. By contrast, a large percentage of Hindus engage with the narratives (generally in their regional language retellings) as religious sources on a regular basis. The narratives, especially the epics, present several characters whose behavior does not always align with the prescriptions of the *dharma* texts. While dharmic prescriptions are stressed generally in epics, in several parts, they are also questioned. The complex dynamics of the *dharma* treatises and the narratives are, therefore, important to keep in view in discussing the basics of Hinduism. Taking the injunctions of the *dharma* treatises as "laws" in the sense of unalterable commandments of Hinduism fails to consider the diverse ways in which they have been interpreted in other important texts that are used regularly by people. Examining intertexual dynamics is vitally important in understanding the basics of Hinduism.

TEXTS ON *dharma* —HUMAN RESPONSIBILITY AND COSMIC ORDER

The term *dharma*, often translated as "law" or "moral code," has no exact equivalent in English. A key and layered concept in all major religious traditions that originated in India –Hinduism, Buddhism, Jainism, and Sikhism – *dharma* has different connotations in each. But all of them are in some way linked to the concept of a moral order that holds all existence together. In this broad sense, it has great cultural currency in India where it has also come to mean "religion" in general. In the Hindu context, the concept has its roots in the RV (1.22.18). The term is derived from the verb *dhṛ* – "to hold together." In early *dharma* literature, it refers to Vedic rituals that were understood to emulate the cosmic order. Several genres of Vedic texts gave detailed instructions for performing public and domestic rituals for the well-being of the society and family. But gradually, the connotations of *dharma* came also to include proper social and moral behavior in texts called *dharma sūtras* and *dharma śāstras*. With a preoccupation with an orderly universe and by extension ordered society, in the Vedic culture, a great deal of effort was made to classify people, foods, time, and space in various broad and minute pure/auspicious and impure/inauspicious categories that would make a functioning system. Proper behavior was conceptualized in relation to one's position in the social system, the stage of one's life as well as the time and place of a moral choice.

Like the Vedic corpus, *dharma* texts are focused on the idea of an individual's responsibility in maintaining order and harmony in the society and the universe. By the time of their composition, the division of the society into four hereditary hierarchical classes of people (called *varṇas*) – priests, warriors, merchants, and servants – had been established. With increasing complexity of the sociopolitical context, however, several communities following diverse professions were integrated into the *varṇa* grid. Each community

was called a *jāti* (from *jāta*, meaning "born"), which was endogamous and was loosely aligned to one category in the *varṇa* hierarchy. The *dharma* texts indicate that the writers considered division
and hierarchy based on the principle of purity as natural and necessary for the cosmic and social order. Those dealing with dead animals or human waste were seen as lowest in the scale of purity and
those dealing with words and rituals as the highest. The treatises on
dharma mostly focused on the obligations of the male members of
the top two *varṇas* – priests (Brahmins) and warriors (Kshatriyas) –
and to an extent those of traders and craftsmen (Vaishyas) – all of
whom also had access to Vedic education. Their *dharma* was related
to their hereditary profession and the goals for an ideal life to be
achieved in its four phases – celibate student, householder, retiree,
and renouncer.

Servants (Shudras), people born of mixed marriages, and those
in professions dealing with dead humans or animals (considered
extremely polluted and therefore "untouchable") did not have
access to Vedic education. Some sections of well-known texts like
Manu Dharmaśāstra (also called *Manu-smṛti*) attributed to the legendary sage Manu had harsh pronouncements stripping these
groups of their human dignity. Social obligations based on hereditary caste hierarchies as laid out in the *dharma śāstra*s have certainly
formed a basis for gross social injustice for centuries. They have
been rightly critiqued in scholarship and public discourses alike.
The abiding influence of the texts, however, appears puzzling in
view of some of their aspects. First, some texts, perhaps compiled
over time, contain apparently contradictory injunctions that are
impossible to follow simultaneously. For example, one chapter in
Manu's text declares that only those households are happy where
women are respected; but another denounces women as frivolous
and asks men to keep them under severe control. Second, while the
tone of the *dharma śāstra*s is authoritative, their injunctions are not
binding commandments. That the authors of the *dharma śāstra*s
themselves were conscious that their injunctions did not have absolute authority is evident in the diverse sources of *dharma* they list.
Manu's text (2.12) lists four sources: the Vedas, the tradition (*smṛti*),
examples of virtuous people, and what is pleasing to one's conscience. Further, the texts mention that the prescribed injunctions,

though generally valid, may be modified according to contexts. As Wendy Doniger has shown, *dharma* as conceptualized in Manu's text is context sensitive and the text tries to cover maximum possible situations/contexts. Finally, average Hindus do not engage with the *dharma* treatises in their religious life. Therefore, their continued influence on Hindu social order is perplexing.

Attention to proper behavior of diverse groups in a range of situations in *dharma* texts often creates an impression that Hinduism lacks universal ethical codes. However, as scholars point out, with the predilection of the *dharma śāstras* toward the priestly class, universal ethics are prescribed most clearly in relation to priests who were their main readers and custodians. For example, Manu's text lays out restrain over senses (2.88), non-harm to all beings in thought, speech, and action (2.161), humility (2.162), hospitality (3.106), compassion (3.113), lack of greed (3.109), etc. for a priest. These injunctions may be followed by all; but if one's occupation does not allow one to always follow them (non-violence for a warrior, for example), this is not a moral failing for the person.

In addition to the *dharma* texts, works emerging from the era that have influenced theologies in various branches of Hinduism and worldviews of people belong to the six schools of Hindu philosophy (*ṣad-darśan*) mentioned earlier – Nyāya, Vaiśeṣṣika, Sāṃkhya, Mimāṃsā, Yoga, and Vedānta. These schools accept the authority of the Vedas; but not all of them accept the existence of a supreme divine and are diverse in their perspectives. Some important Hindu concepts they discuss are: (a) consciousness and matter (broadly identified as male and female principles *puruṣa* and *prakṛti*) as constituting the world; and *sattva* (goodness, harmoniousness), *rajas* (passion, activeness), and *tamas* (darkness, chaos) as three qualities found in different degrees in all things and persons; (b) meditation and spiritual discipline; (c) logic as basis of knowledge; and (d) liberation through self-realization. Even though important, these texts have remained a matter of specialized studies. An extremely important philosophical text of this era is Badarayan's *Brahma Sūtra* (ca fourth century), which systematically summarizes the spiritual teachings of the Upanishads in pithy verses. This text was grouped together with the Upanishads and the *Bhagavad Gita* as forming *prasthāntrayi* (three axioms for philosophical departure).

In the subsequent centuries, major *advaita* (non-dualist) philosophers like Adi Shankara (eighth century) and theologians like
Ramanuja (eleventh century) wrote commentaries on *prasthāntrayi*
to establish their schools of thought.

NARRATIVES

Of all the Sanskrit texts originating in the ancient period, two
epics – the *Ramayana* and the *Mahabharata* – as well as a myriad
of stories about deities contained in the Puranas have been most
integrated in the lives of average Hindus for centuries. These
texts interweave narratives from priestly, bardic, and regional
traditions that may have been in oral circulation much earlier.
Even today, people generally do not read the narratives but listen
to them in regional versions. There are indeed hundreds of
retellings of these narratives with diverse interpretations. A vast
majority of Hindu children get their early religious lessons
through these stories.

   The narrative texts emerged when the Vedic culture was facing
major challenges from other traditions. If the *dharma* treatises
responded to the challenges by defining moral obligations of
people, the narrative texts did so in three important ways. First,
characters in them provided examples of how to engage with issues
of *dharma*. Second, they contributed to the development of the
pantheon of deities who have been widely worshiped by Hindus
for centuries. And third, they democratized the tradition by
popularizing the path of *bhakti*, which, unlike Vedic rituals or mystical knowledge, was open to all. Over the centuries, they have
indeed provided Hindu communities what Gananath Obeyesekere
has termed "myth models," filters to distill meanings from human
experience. They have also provided the basis for numerous literary,
visual, and performing arts in classical and folk traditions. When
Hindu traditions traveled to South-East Asia in the early Common
Era, the narratives formed a major channel for their integration
into local cultures, often through sculptures and performing arts
that are popular even today. Additionally, the settings of the narratives allowed various locales of the subcontinent to be integrated
into Hindu pilgrimage networks.

The Epics

Two epics – the *Ramayana* and the *Mahabharata* – are considered sacred by Hindus and are traditionally classified as *itihāsa* ("so indeed it happened"). Of these, the *Ramayana*, attributed to sage Valmiki, is 24,000 verses long. It tells the story of the righteous prince Rama of Ayodhya who accepts a 14-year long exile from his kingdom on the eve of his coronation in order to enable his father to fulfill a promise made to his stepmother. In exile, Rama is accompanied by his wife Sita and brother Lakshman. Sita, whom king Janaka had found in a furrow and raised as a princess, is extremely beautiful. She is abducted from their forest hut and kept captive for months by the ten-headed king Ravana. But she refuses to submit to Ravana's demands. Rama and Lakshman go looking for her. On the way, they befriend valiant forest dwellers and monkeys who help them find her and fight as Rama's army in the subsequent battle against Ravana. Hanuman, their chief, becomes an ardent devotee of Rama. When Ravana is slain and Rama is victorious, Sita approaches Rama happily; but he asks her to prove her chastity. Sita enters fire; and the fire deity, Agni, brings her back unharmed testifying to her chastity. Rama, Sita, and Lakshman return to Ayodhya and Rama is crowned the king. The final turn is introduced in the last book of the epic, which is generally seen as a later addition. Soon after the coronation, on hearing rumors about Sita's time in Ravana's city circulating among his subjects, Rama banishes a pregnant Sita to the forest. Here, sage Valmiki, the author of the epic, gives her shelter in his hermitage. Sita gives birth to twin sons – Luv and Kush – and raises them there. Valmiki teaches them his poem, the *Ramayana*, which they recite in Rama's city Ayodhya at the performance of a major sacrifice. Rama recognizes his sons, Valmiki brings Sita in front of Rama who is moved to see her. But Sita does not want to return. She asks the earth, her mother (since she was found in a furrow), to accept her back. The ground splits and Sita disappears into it.

The *Ramayana* is focused on the issue of *dharma* of a son, a king, a wife, a brother, a friend, etc. But it also deals with complex moral dilemmas faced by the characters and does not portray any of them as blemish-free. Rama's choices in a few incidents have been a

matter of debates. His asking Sita to prove her purity and abandon-
ing her when pregnant, which led to her poignant return to mother
earth are two such incidents. On the other hand, Ravana, even
though arrogant and boastful, is portrayed to have some good qualities. He does not force himself on Sita, is immensely learned and a
great devotee of Shiva. His fatal flaw is arrogance. The issues of
dharma in the *Ramayana* continue to be debated in public discourses, writings, and performances within Hindu communities
and by non-Hindus in India and outside of it. The debates among
Hindus highlight that diverse perspectives are valid in the Hindu
ethos. People may bitterly disagree; but critiquing Rama's behavior
is not sacrilege. In addition to being a resource for *dharma* related
issues, the *Ramayana* is one of the most significant texts for *bhakti*
traditions. There are millions of ardent devotees of Rama, who is
often seen flanked by Sita, and Laxman in his iconography. Equally
popular is Hanuman, seen as divine because of his devotion, even
though taking a monkey body. Deep attachment to Rama however
has become a part of sharp political debates in recent decades,
which we will look at later.

The other epic, attributed to sage Dwaipayan Vyasa, is the
Mahabharata. Arguably the longest epic in the world, it is almost
five times as long as the *Ramayana* and even a more complex net
of stories involving *dharma* choices. The main narrative is about
rivalry between two sets of cousins – 100 Kauravas and
5 Pandavas – to inherit a powerful kingdom. The Kauravas
refuse to share power with the Pandavas and put them through a
series of life-threatening ordeals including a long exile imposed
through a tricky game of gambling. Contributing vitally to the
complexity of the tale is the role of princess Draupadi, who is
married to all five Pandavas. She is enraged when Kauravas drag
her to their court and attempt to strip her during the game as a
bet and is determined to avenge her insult. Pandavas lose everything and are forced to exile. After many years in exile, the
Pandavas enter an epic battle with the Kauravas with Krishna
(worshipped as another incarnation of Vishnu) on their side, not
as a warrior but as an advisor. After a devastatingly destructive
war, the Pandavas emerge victorious but are gripped with a deep
sense of loss. In the end, as they embark on their last journey to

heaven along with Draupadi, each of them, except the eldest Yudhishthira, is made to confront his/her flaws before he/she falls. There are hundreds of stories surrounding the main plot, each presenting a moral dilemma faced by a character. Here too, no character is painted as perfect.

Moral choices and their consequences are presented with stark realism and a range of possibilities in the *Mahabharata*. Draupadi, a princess, marries five brothers to follow the word of their mother. On the other hand, another princess, Amba, rebels when pressured to marry a man she does not love. She turns an ascetic, gets reborn as a prince with fluid gender, and becomes instrumental in the death of the person who had abducted her in the previous life. Some choices of various characters align with injunctions of the *dharma śāstras*, and some do not. In several situations, the choices of authoritative figures are questioned or shown in poor light. In the episode where Draupadi is being dragged into the court by the Kauravas, she sharply questions the male elders of the family for choosing loyalty to the throne over their duty to protect a woman. In another subplot, Ekalavya, a young forest-dweller who excels in archery, is tricked by the royal teacher Drona (a Brahmin) whom he considers his guru. On discovering Eklavya's extraordinary skills, Drona asks Ekalavya to give him his (Ekalvya's) right thumb as his fee. This is a trick to ensure that Arjun, one of the Pandavas, remains the greatest archer in the world. As Ekalavya devotedly cuts his thumb, the cruelty of the Brahmin teacher and the nobility of the forest-dweller (considered low caste) become transparent. This story is told with myriad different interpretations. A Dalit leader, for example, recently commented that in cutting his thumb, Eklavya, though showing nobility, allowed Drona to hit at the source of his skills.

Heard in summary or piecemeal, the epics are seen by average Hindus as important sources of guidance regarding moral choices. But as narratives, they provide no straightforward injunctions. They rather present diverse situations, which reinforce the idea that while some values such as kindness, truthfulness, etc. are universal, moral decisions are often complex and must be made in view of their contexts. Within a complex web of such stories, however, there is one important interlude in the *Mahabharata*, generally thought to be a later addition, that is regarded as a core Hindu text – the famous *Bhagavad Gita*.

The Bhagavad Gita

Of all the Hindu sacred texts, the *Bhagavad Gita* ("the song of the Lord") or the *Gita* (BG now on) is the best known worldwide. Perhaps the author/s of BG inserted it into the *Mahabharata* because of the epic's popularity. Like the Upanishads, this text is in the form of a dialog. It clearly tries to synthesize all major philosophical/spiritual ideas prevalent at the time. A large majority of its 700 verses, divided into 18 chapters, are about various perspectives on the real nature of the self, its relation to the divine, the nature of the Ultimate, and the characteristics of a spiritually advanced person. The text lays out three paths of spiritual advancement – undertaking action for the fulfillment of duties without attachment to results (*niṣkām karma*), surrender to the divine will in devotion(*bhakti*), and knowledge of the self (*jnāna*) – which are still seen as major religious paths by Hindus.

Along with the ideas it contains, the narrative context of BG also demands attention. It is placed in the epic when the battle is about to begin. Arjun, the mightiest warrior on the Pandava side, is overcome by dejection at the prospect of killing relatives and friends. He expresses his doubts to Krishna, his guide. In the dialog that follows, Krishna advises Arjun to give up his doubts arising out of confusion and fulfill his *dharma* as a warrior by fighting for what is right. The text ends with Arjun saying, "I will do as you say." Because of this narrative context, some readers interpret BG as advocating war and being apathetic to destruction. Yet millions who turn to it as a source of spiritual guidance, see the narrative context of the battle only as a symbol of the inner struggle of a person, which highlights the spiritual message of the text. They view Krishna's exhortation to Arjun to fight not as a justification for war but as a call to perform one's duty without any expectation of a reward. In a lecture I attended, a teacher of BG said, "It is important to keep in mind that Krishna asks Arujn, a warrior who has already arrived on the battlefield, to fight and not an ordinary citizen. Arjun here is like the commander-in-chief of an army refusing to perform his job. He has to be exhorted to fulfill his duty." Because of the understanding that BG's teaching is about performing righteous action without attachment to its fruits, it is regarded as a pivotal sacred text by most Hindus. Even during the COVID-19 pandemic, many Hindus were exchanging verses from it on social media channels discussing the need to introspect on collective *karma* and perform one's duty in the battle against the virus.

THE PURANAS

Along with the epics, the other core narrative texts of Hinduism are the Puranas, a truly large corpus. These texts were composed over several centuries beginning in the early Common Era. Eighteen Puranas are considered *Mahāpurāṇa*s (great Puranas) and are attributed to the same legendary sage Vyasa to whom the *Mahabharata* is ascribed. They are encyclopedic in scope and generally weave five themes – cosmogony, dissolution and recreation of the world in a cyclical manner within vast expanses of time spanning millions of years, life on earth during these cycles, myths about deities and their worshippers, and genealogies and deeds of royal dynasties. Several widely prevalent Hindu ideas about how humans and deities are situated within these cycles of creation and dissolution derive from these texts.

Manu, the name of the progenitor of mankind in Hindu belief, also appears in the Puranas. Here, it is the title of the upholder of the world whose lifetime spans thousands of years within cycles of time. As per the conception of time presented in the Puranas, lifetimes of 14 Manus make one iteration of creation with its own distinct deities. During the lifetime of each Manu, the world goes through a cycle of four eons (*yugas*) – *kṛta/satya, tretā, dvāpar*, and *kali* – each of several thousand years. In a cycle of this type, called *mahāyuga*, there is gradual moral degradation from the first eon, *kṛta*, which is marked by moral uprightness of people. The cycles of human rebirths are set within this complex schema of time. Hindus often find explanations for moral corruption in the world today by associating it with the current degenerate *kali-yuga*. Generally, a Purana presents *bhakti* to the deity at its center as the most efficacious path for liberation in the *kali-yuga*. Devotional practices dedicated to popular deities in the current times – with specific rituals, festivals, and pilgrimage – are largely based on these texts. The Puranas can be seen as sourcebooks of several aspects of Hinduism as prevalent today – theology, devotional practices, and understandings of time and space.

The Puranic corpus synthesized components of old priestly worldview, concepts from Vedic texts, bardic tales of heroes, and worship of regional non-Vedic deities, contributing to Hinduism's recovery from the setbacks given by devotional currents in traditions like Buddhism. The roots of the process of "vernacularization," which we will discuss in the next chapter, can be seen in the synthesis occurring in this corpus. This resulted in a major shift in the Hindu pantheon. Vedic gods like Indra and Agni receded in significance and three deities with rich and more relatable human traits came to occupy central positions. This shift parallels Buddhist and Jain literature, where too, Vedic deities appear as subordinate to the Buddha and the Jain teachers. The Hindu deities who became prominent with the Puranas were: Vishnu with his several incarnations, Shiva with multiple manifestations, and the great goddess, Mahadevi, in her many forms embodying the cosmic energy (*śakti*). Several regional deities were integrated into the mythologies of these expanding the pantheon that was flexible in its boundaries and yet has remained stable for close to two millennia. The process of integration of regional or local deities into broader Hindu pantheon through narratives in regional languages is still ongoing.

Almost every major Purana has a specific deity at the center who is identified as a manifestation of the Supreme entity (variously called Prajapati, Purusa, or Brahman in the Vedic literature). But other deities also populate its mythical world, not as rivals but as associates or members of family who acknowledge the supreme status of the deity at the center. Each of them has a distinctive personality, unique emblems, and a bird or an animal as *vāhana* (vehicle to ride). The myths present the main deity (and others) as full of grace and protective of her/his human or animal devotees. Personal devotion or *bhakti* to the deity is highlighted as the most efficacious religious path leading to the attainment of liberation from the cycles of birth. It is open to all – including women and those considered low caste, who were generally excluded from paths of liberation through Vedic knowledge. Importantly, devotional practices described in the Puranas also draw on non-Vedic philosophical and esoteric currents that had been prevalent in the subcontinent. One such current is Tantra, which is marked by a view of the material universe as sacred and the use of the human body and mantras for spiritual progress. Tantric influence is especially pronounced in the worship of the goddess. The shift from centrality of Vedic deities who were offered fire sacrifices by priests to incorporation of regional deities into the pantheon and non-Vedic elements into worship practices available to all, popularized the tradition to a large degree.

Puranas have served as important texts for several sects that arose around popular deities. *Viṣṇu* and *Bhāgavat* Puranas are important texts for Vaishnava (Vishnu devotion) sects; *Linga* and *Śiva* for sects dedicated to Shiva; and the *Devī Mahātmya*, a section of the *Mārkaṇḍeya Purāṇa* for sects devoted to the goddess. Yet, vast masses of Hindus who engage regularly with mythologies in these texts remain non-sectarian and worship multiple deities seeing them as different manifestations of the One Ultimate that permeates all existence.

POPULAR HINDU DEITIES SINCE THE PURANIC ERA

Vishnu, Shiva, and the goddess are the most prominent deities in the Puranic texts. But because creation and dissolution of the world is a core theme in the Puranas, in addition to these individual deities, a triad (*trimurti*) of three male deities – Brahma, Vishnu, and Shiva – appears in several narratives as responsible for creation, preservation, and dissolution of the world, respectively. Of these, Brahma (a deity and not Brahman, the Ultimate reality) is generally linked to the powerful Vedic god Prajapati who was identified as the creator. In the Puranas, he often appears as arising from the navel of Vishnu. He is described as having four heads (each facing a direction) and four hands, holding the Vedas, a rosary, a lotus, and a water pot (sometimes a scepter). His *vāhana* is the swan. He is referred as the Lord of the Vedas; and he is related to the goddess of knowledge Saraswati (sometimes as consort and sometimes as father). But gradually, Brahma lost in popularity. Today, only a few temples dedicated to Brahma are found, whereas there are innumerable temples of Vishnu, Shiva, and the goddess.

VISHNU

Vishnu ("the pervader") is mentioned in the RV as a minor deity associated with powerful Indra, the sun, and its movements. But since the rise of Puranic corpus, he is worshipped as a major deity associated with preservation of the universe. Several of the *Mahāpurāṇas* – *Vishnu*, *Garuda*, *Bhāgavata*, and *Varāha* – are dedicated to him. The most significant part of Vishnu's mythology is the concept of *avatār* or divine descent on earth. Vishnu descends on earth from his celestial abode in an animal or human form whenever life on earth or *dharma* is in danger. In his celestial form, Vishnu is generally depicted as reclining on the endless serpent Shesha on the milky ocean. In this depiction, his consort Lakshmi, the goddess of well-being and prosperity, is often seen massaging his legs. His *vāhana* (vehicle) is Garuda (eagle). But his descents on the earth appear in many forms. Their multiplicity, as found in the Puranas, allowed some popular narratives and regional deities to be incorporated into the Hindu ethos. Ten of these (with some variations in lists) collectively called *daśāvatāra* (ten descents) have widely popular narratives and often (but now always) appear in the following order. (The names of the first five are in italics because they are words with specific meanings.)

1. *Matsya* (fish) – In a myth paralleling the great deluge narratives in many traditions of the world such as that of Noah, Vishnu descended as a small fish that grew giant and saved its progenitor and creatures of the world by carrying their boat to safe shores.
2. *Kurma* (tortoise) – When powerful gods and non-gods churned the ocean for its treasures, Vishnu provided a firm basis for the churning staff in the form of a tortoise.

3. *Varāha* (boar) – When a demon dragged the Earth (imagined as a woman) to the bottom of the cosmic ocean, taking the form of a boar, Vishnu rescued her.

4. *Narasiṃha* (man-lion) – Vishnu appeared as half-lion half-man to rescue his true devotee Prahalada who was tortured by his father for following *bhakti*.

5. *Vāmana* (dwarf) – When the invincible king Bali's power threatened the cosmic order, Vishnu appeared as a child and asked for a gift of territory measuring his three steps. When his request was granted, he took his cosmic form and measured the three worlds in three steps to reestablish order.

6. Parashuram – In a fully human form, Vishnu protected Brahmins oppressed by Kshatriya men. Parashuram annihilated all Kshatriya men, sparing only the ones who were still in their mothers' wombs.

7. Rama – Vishnu descended as a prince of Ayodhya (the hero of the *Rāmāyana*) to provide a model of righteous behavior.

8. Krishna – In the next human descent as Krishna, Vishnu was born in a royal clan, but in prison since his parents were imprisoned by his uncle. He was taken miraculously to a cowherd community for safety and grew up with his foster parents as a pampered and naughty child. He developed bonds of love with the cowherds (especially with cowherd women with whom he danced and had amorous relations), even as he protected them from a variety of mishaps with his divine powers. These are some of the most popular Hindu narratives. Krishna also took the role of the spiritual guide in BG. In his iconography, he is generally seen as a youthful figure playing the flute under a tree. But sometimes he is also seen as Arjuna's teacher and charioteer in the battlefield.

9. Buddha – Vishnu appeared as the popular spiritual teacher to teach about nonviolence (sometimes presented as a compassionate teacher and sometimes as the one who led demons to follow the *nāstik* path). (While the Buddha's appearance in the list may seem unusual in contemporary times, in ancient India, the appearance of the same divine figures in different religious traditions was not unusual. Indra and Brahma appear in Buddhist narratives too, in subordinate roles compared to the Buddha.)

10. Kalki – As a future *avatāra* of Vishnu, Kalki is prophesied to
bring about the end of *kali yuga* and usher the morally perfect
kṛta. He is depicted as riding a white horse and having a sword
in a hand.

The most popular *avatāra*s of Vishnu are Rama and Krishna.
Their popularity derives to a great degree from their relatability at
the human level. Rama is an exemplar of *dharmic* life for many.
Krishna inspires adoration as a child, intense love as a friend or
lover, and reverence as the teacher of BG. Several sects of devotion
to Vishnu or one of his *avatāra*s (especially to Rama and Krishna)
have developed in various parts of India since the late first millennium. A prominent sect that has developed outside of India is
International Society of Krishna Consciousness (ISKCON) to be
discussed later. In these Vaishnava sects, Vishnu or a specific *avatār*
of his is worshipped as the Supreme – *parabrahman* – and other deities as subordinate to him. He is also the inner dweller of the human
heart who knows all thoughts stirring within a devotee. Pilgrimage sites and festivals associated with Vishnu and his *avatār*s also
form important parts of Hindu cultural ethos. Chaitrali, whom we
met in the Introduction, was teaching dance to poor children for
performance based on Krishna's narratives.

SHIVA

Even though in the "Hindu triad," Shiva is the lord of dissolution
(not destruction) at the end of a cycle of creation, his name means
"auspicious." The major Puranas focusing on him are *Vāyu*, *Śiva*,
and *Linga*. In his divine aspects, Shiva is linked to Vedic deity
Rudra, an associate of Vayu (wind) who is praised as powerful.
Rudra is recognized as the Lord in YV and the *Śvetāśvatara* Upanishad. However, Shiva's exalted divine status, marked by an enig-
matic mystical aura and deep paradox, gets fully established in the
Puranas. He is praised here as the greatest of yogis meditating on
the Himalayan peak Kailash. But he is also portrayed as enjoying
prolonged erotic union with his wife Parvati. The divine couple is
represented in temples with an aniconic image of male and female
union. The subtitle of Wendy Doniger's book on Shiva "The Erotic

Ascetic" aptly captures this paradox. As a yogi, he possesses nothing. Yet even with his mendicant status, he is a happy family man with two sons. Parvati is his second wife. A myth about the death of his first wife Sati (herself a manifestation of the great goddess), a daughter of Brahmā's son King Daksha, is one of the central ones in Shaivite mythology. According to it, Sati's father had organized a grand sacrifice and had invited all powerful gods and goddesses, but out of embarrassment of having an ascetic son-in-law who possessed nothing, he did not invite Shiva. An enraged Sati reached her father's palace and immolated herself. Shiva was distraught. He first destroyed the sacrifice and then carried her body around the world, indifferent to his divine duties. In order to shake him out of this state, Vishnu cut parts of Sati's body that fell in different parts of the Indian subcontinent which became pilgrimage centers for the goddess. Shiva came out of his trance. Sati was reborn as Parvati, the daughter of the king of mountains Himalaya, and was married to Shiva. The Puranas portray him as a deity who is easily pleased; but his rage can destabilize the world. He sits withdrawn from the world and looking inward; but he is the lord of dance. He does not have earthly descents like Vishnu, but each member of his family is a deity in their own right; and he has a large entourage of assistants.

In his anthropomorphic iconography, Shiva is generally seen sitting in deep meditation, very much like the Buddha. His throat has a bluish mark, and his long hair is matted. He is clad in the hide of a tiger; wears the crescent moon in his hair; has snakes encircling his arms and neck; and has the river Ganga flowing from his matted hair. At times, he is also seen sitting in his Himalayan abode with his family. By his side is seen his *vāhana* Nandi, the bull. Each element of his iconography has a related myth. The myth of the Ganga (the holiest of rivers for Hindus) flowing from his hair, for example, relates how when the forceful flow of the river descended from heaven, it was feared that the earth would not be able to endure it. Shiva caught the river in his matted hair and channeled it on the earth with controlled force. According to another myth, when the superhuman groups, *sura*s and *asura*s, churned the cosmic ocean to get the nectar of immortality, one of the first things to come out was immeasurably potent poison. No one wanted it. Shiva gulped it to prevent it from dropping on the earth and stopped it in his throat, which became blue-tinged. Along with Shiva's image as a yogi, one of his most important anthropomorphic forms, especially in South India, is that of Nataraja (the lord of dance), where he is depicted in a dancing pose in a ring of flames and with a hand drum. In this pose, he is the master of all movements in the cosmos, setting time in motion with his drum.

Shiva and Parvati have two sons – Skanda/Kartikeya and Ganesha, both born miraculously. Kartikeya is a warrior deity, worshipped in South India as Murugan (who was likely a regional deity earlier). As per narratives, he was born of the spilled seed of Śiva carried in the waters of the Ganga and was nurtured by six nymphs. When he grew up, he killed the demon Tarka. In his iconography he appears as the handsome warrior god with weapons like spear, bows, and arrow and his *vāhana*, the peacock. Ganesha, the other son of Shiva, is perhaps the most ubiquitous presence – in homes, businesses, restaurants, and dorm rooms – among Hindu divinities. This elephant-headed deity with a potbelly is worshipped as the remover of obstacles. In his iconography, he is often seen with sweets in front of him; and a broken tusk, an axe, a noose, and sometimes with a pen or a lotus in hands (Hindu gods generally have several hands indicating their supernatural status). As per his mythology, he was created by Parvati on her own when Shiva was away for meditation. When Shiva returned, young Ganesha tried to stop him from approaching Parvati. In anger, Shiva cut his head. But when Parvati reproached Shiva, he revived Ganesha by putting an elephant's head on him. Ganesha, originally a non-Vedic deity, is thus incorporated in the pantheon and is one of the most popular deities among Hindus today. He is also widely known among non-Hindus since his images are found frequently in restaurants and business locations.

ŚAKTI AND THE GODDESSES

The third important cluster of divinities in the Hindu pantheon that expanded through narrative literature and has continued to grow in a layered manner is that of goddesses, all of whom are worshipped as manifestations of *śakti*, the cosmic energy conceptualized as feminine. In view of ardent worshippers of the goddess, this energy sets the universe in motion and permeates all life. As the active aspect of the Ultimate, it is complementary to the more detached self-absorbed aspect of consciousness, conceptualized as masculine.

Goddesses such as Ushas (dawn), Vac (inspiring speech), Saraswati (river and nourisher) are found even in RV; but they are not as numerous or powerful as their male counterparts. A fully developed theology of the divine feminine with several goddesses as forms of śakti or its personalized form – Mahadevi – is found only in later texts such as the Puranas. This difference is viewed in different ways in scholarship. Some scholars hold that in the patriarchal Vedic worldview, goddesses had little significance. They see the dynamic goddess traditions developing almost exclusively because of the incorporation of elements from non-Aryan Tantric and regional traditions. On the other hand, Tracy Pintchman suggests that even though vague, a sense of "feminine principle" operative in the universe emerges from interrelated aspects of Vedic goddesses. David Kinsley observes that even though lacking well-developed personalities, many Vedic divine feminine figures have aspects that get transferred to goddesses whose traditions developed with the Puranas. Aspects of Vac as sacred speech, for example, are transferred to Saraswati as the goddess of learning (not the Vedic river). Another aspect of Vedic mythology that continues in the Puranas is the role of female deities as consorts of male divine beings. However, in the Puranas, the feminine principle becomes endowed with great power. The consort goddesses are the source of power of their male partners. There are also some independent goddesses who are even more formidable than their male counterparts.

The most important text about powerful independent goddesses is a section of the *Mārkandeya* Purana titled the *Devī Mahatmya* (glory of the goddess, ca sixth century), which contains the narrative about Durga. According to it, once the gods and demons were in a long battle over the control of the world. The army of demons was led by the buffalo headed Mahishasura who was invincible and was creating havoc in the world. When a host of deities approached Vishnu, Shiva, and Brahma, they were enraged, and their energy blazed forth from their forms. Energy of all other divine beings also came out of their bodies. The combined energies of all divine beings took a splendid female form. This was Durga. All gods gave her their respective weapons and honored her. In the ferocious battle that followed, from the enraged Durga's brow, emerged ferocious goddess Kali. Durga finally slayed Mahishasura. This mythological moment is represented widely in art and the battle forms the basis of the festival of nine nights – Navaratri. Numerous regional and village goddesses around India are worshipped as full or partial manifestations of Durga.

Among the consort goddesses, who are generally gentle, the most important are: Lakshmi, the consort of Vishnu, Parvati, Shiva's consort, and Saraswati, Brahma's consort. In Lakshmi's myth, she emerges as one of jewels emerging from the churning of the ocean by gods and non-gods. She becomes Vishnu's bride. She is worshipped with Vishnu; but also, by herself as the goddess of prosperity and the giver of all auspicious things, especially during the festival of Diwali. Parvati is the reincarnation of Shiva's first wife Sati. In her mythology, Parvati wins over Shiva, who is indifferent to her beauty, by performing great asceticism. She has a calming effect on him. And even though he is her guru, she has a relatively equal relationship with him, represented in iconography of *ardhanārīshvara* (half woman lord) as the left half of Shiva. Saraswatī, the Vedic goddess with river-like attributes, offers an early example of veneration of waters and land in Hinduism. But in the Puranas, she is associated with intelligence, speech, the arts, and culture. Her iconography is the gentlest of goddesses with white attire, a Veena (string instrument), a book and a rosary in hands, and swan as her vehicle. She is worshipped at the beginning of school years and academic endeavors.

It is significant that in the Puranas, Brahma, the Lord of the Vedas, recedes in significance. This can be seen as a dynamic reconfiguration of the ritual centered Vedic religion in response to the popularity of the devotional current in Buddhism, which had challenged Brahminical authority. In the epics and Puranas, individuals from the priestly class appear sometimes as good but minor characters, and sometimes in poor light. No central character of the epics or Purana is Brahmin. Vishnu's *avatār*s Rama and Krishna as well as the Pandavas are Kshatriya princes (as was Siddharth, the later Buddha); and Shiva is a mountain dweller. Whereas Ravana, the abductor of Sita in the *Ramayana*, and Drona, who gets Ekalavya's thumb cut in the *Mahabharata*, are Brahmins. Ascetic Shiva's destruction of Daksha's sacrifice can also be seen as a powerful myth of the shift away from priestly rituals and authority. Hindu narratives however, retain the centrality of householder life as upheld by the Vedic culture. They depict the deities in happy conjugal relations with their divine consorts. The narratives became immensely popular because of the ways in which they modified and expanded the divine pantheon. The myths of deities with well-defined and relatable personalities with whom human devotees from various layers of the society interacted circulated widely. Their diverse interpretations became prevalent and their appeal to the masses pumped a new life into the religious culture that still honored the Vedas, if ceremoniously. It is important to note again that in this process the non-Brahminical and non-Vedic contributions were vital. The reconfigured ethos had all the important features of Hinduism as it prevails today. While the narratives played a core role in this process, they did not reach all layers of the society through Sanskrit manuscripts. They reached the masses through retellings in regional languages, many of which were in performative genres and have remained vibrantly alive for centuries. To those texts, which form a part of the cluster of channels through which core values and concepts contained in the formative texts are filtered to the broader Hindu society, we turn in the next chapter.

Table 2.1 Sacred Texts in Sanskrit

Texts	Enduring influence
Vedic *saṃhitā*s	• Validity of multiple voices • View of nature as sacred • Human responsibility in maintaining order in the cosmos (expressed in ritual *karma*) • Centrality of householder life
Upanishads	• Brahman as the Ultimate underlying reality of all existence, identity of individual self – *ātman* – with Brahman • Focus on inner search for self-realization • *Jnāna* as more important than ritual performance

(Continued)

Table 2.1 Sacred Texts in Sanskrit *(Continued)*

Texts	Enduring influence
Dharma literature	• Individual's responsibility toward family and society • Stratification of a hierarchical order of society on the *varṇa* and *jāti* grid with severe discrimination against the lowest castes and Dalits ("untouchables") • Moral duties aligned to position in the society • Recognition of significance of context in moral choices • Restrictions on women, confining her life to family duties • Stress on values of truthfulness, honesty, and kindness
Epics	• Examples of complex moral choices through relatable human characters • Stress on moral duty to others • The *Bhagavad Gita* • Network of narratives later transmitted through oral traditions in regional languages with diverse interpretations • Basis for a range of visual and performative arts
Puranas	• Expansion of the pantheon of deities with integration of non-Vedic and regional deities (a process that continues even today) • Validity of emotions in religious experience through *bhakti* • Relatable narratives about deities for all strata of the society • Basis for several sectarian traditions • Alignment to temple culture with iconography embedded in narratives • Basis for visual and performative arts

FURTHER EXPLORATION SUGGESTIONS

Brook, Peters et al., dirs. 2001. *The Mahabharata*. DVD. London: Channel Four Television Company.

Debroy, Bibek, trans. 2015. *The Mahabharata*. Gurgaon, Haryana, India: Penguin Books.

Dimmitt, Cornelia, and J. A. B. van Buitenen. 1978. *Classical Hindu Mythology: A Reader in the Sanskrit Purāṇas*. Philadelphia, PA: Temple University Press.

Eknath, Easwaran. 2019. *The Bhagavad Gita*, 2nd ed. Classics of Indian Spirituality. Tomales, CA: Nilgiri Press.

Jamison, Stephanie W., and Joel P. Brereton, trans. 2017. *The Rigveda: The Earliest Religious Poetry of India*. South Asia Research. New York, NY: Oxford University Press.

Manu. 1991. *The Laws of Manu*. translation and Introduction by Wendy Doniger and Brian Smith. London, England: Penguin.

Moghe, Gauri. 2021. "Upanishads: The Essence of Vedic Philosophy." Video. Pune: Bhandarkar Oriental Institute. https://www.youtube.com/watch?v=HmTYhLnVdQ8. Accessed on July 3, 2022.

Olivelle, Patrick. 2009. *Dharma: Studies in Its Semantic, Cultural, and Religious History*. Delhi: Motilal Banarsidass.

Vālmīki, and Ramesh Menon. 2004. *The Ramayana*. First North Point Press paperback ed. New York, NY: North Point Press.

3

FUNCTIONAL SACRED TEXTS
Vernacular Performativity

In the last chapter, we looked at Hindu sacred texts in Sanskrit composed between 1500 BCE and the end of the first millennium of the Common Era, which often incorporated non-Vedic and non-Sanskrit regional religious elements too as the Hindu ethos spread in various parts of present-day South Asia. Even though numerous texts in entirety and large portions of many are now lost, a vast corpus of Sanskrit sacred writings has been preserved by the elite and has circulated in all parts of India and Nepal. The contents of many of them, especially the narratives, have inevitably filtered through all layers of the society over the centuries through texts in diverse regional languages of the subcontinent. The dynamics between the pan-Indian Sanskrit and vernacular texts has formed an important basic of Hinduism for the past several centuries. They have indeed provided the woof and warp of Hindu religious life.

The process of exchange between Sanskrit sacred texts and the regional oral texts has most likely gone on since ancient times. As seen earlier, since early phases of classical Hinduism, the contributions of regional elements are more apparent in sacred texts. However, we have much clear evidence and better knowledge of how this interplay generated an ethos of layered authority and agency in the Hindu communities from the last centuries of the first

DOI: 10.4324/9781315303352-4

millennium as some vernacular texts from that era are still alive in performance. These texts relate to the elite texts in various, often paradoxical, ways – translation, reinterpretation, expansion, subversion, or outright challenge. In scholarship on Indian literature, the rise and contributions of vernacular texts with far-reaching implications is termed "vernacularization." At times, it is discussed as first supplementing and eventually replacing the elite literary forms. We will see in this chapter that while this is partially the case, there is also an intentionally maintained continuum between the elite Sanskrit and vernacular genres, which have served as the "functional" or "operative" sacred texts for a large percentage of Hindus. Vernacular texts are found mostly in performative genres: devotional and festival songs, ballads for recitation, narratives for popular rituals, folk plays, sacred biographies of saintly figures, women's songs for life cycle rituals and daily life, etc. People use them freely with or without the presence of priests. The opening up of the Hindu traditions, stirred by incorporation of regional non-Vedic elements in Sanskrit sacred texts, finds its fruition in the usage of vernacular texts by ordinary Hindus in everyday life. They nourish the faith of millions. For this reason, they are equally or perhaps even more mainstream sacred texts than the Sanskrit corpus.

While the sheer enormity of genres of vernacular texts does not allow their comprehensive review here, we will survey a few major categories in this chapter. Regional Hindu sacred texts in India and Nepal belong to different language families such as Indo-Aryan, Dravidian, Sino-Tibetan. Several languages spoken in northern regions of India such as Hindi, Bengali, Marathi, Gujarati, Punjabi, Oriya, and Assamese are Indo-Aryan languages developed in the early second millennium from regional dialects categorized as *apabhraṃśa*, which were rooted in Sanskrit. Nepali too is an Indo-Aryan language. The Dravidian languages – Tamil, Kannada, Telugu, and Malayalam – have ancient roots. Tamil had well-established literary traditions by the early centuries of the Common Era. The languages spoken in some parts of north-east India and Himalayan regions are Sino-Tibetan. These linguistic variations play an important role in Hindu life on the ground. Texts composed in them, ground the religious messages in the specificity of regional culture, making them more relatable for people. Several examples included here come from the Gujarati language because I am able to provide my translations for them. But similar examples in various genres are found abundantly in other languages as well.

VERNACULAR LITERARY VERSIONS OF CLASSICAL SANSKRIT TEXTS

The centrality of vernacular sacred texts in religious routines of Hindu communities is indicated clearly by usage of regional versions of some well-known Sanskrit texts. Two immensely popular and influential retellings of the *Ramayana* are the Tamil *Rāmāvataram* by poet Kamban (between ninth and twelfth centuries) and the *Ramcharitmanas* by Banaras's sixteenth-century poet Tulsidas in Avadhi (a dialect of Hindi). Considered classics in their respective languages, both these versions follow the basic plot of Valmiki's epic. But they differ in their ways of presenting the characters. Kamban's Rama grows gradually into his divine stature. Tulsidas's poem highlights Rama's inherent divinity, Sita's gentleness, and Hanuman's *bhakti*. But it does not have the part of pregnant Sita's exile into the forest. Few people read the *Ramayana* in Sanskrit. But Kamban's poem is recited every year in the Tamil month of Ādi by thousands. In north India, Tulsi's *Ramcharitmanas* is read/recited extensively in the month of Sāvan. And as we will see in the last chapter, it is at the core of religious life for several Hindu communities in the diaspora. Scores of other versions of the epic are extant in regional languages of South and South-east Asia. Another regional text related to a Sanskrit classic is the twelfth-century saint Jnaneshvar's commentary on the *Gita* (BG) in the Marathi language. This text, Jnāneshwari, is also widely popular and is regarded highly as the pivotal literary work in Marathi.

SONGS AND LIVES OF SAINT-POETS

Of all the genres of vernacular Hindu sacred texts, the ones that have received extensive scholarly attention are lyrics and sacred biographies (hagiographies) of poets who composed devotional songs in their regional languages, perhaps because parallels to these are also found in Islamic Sufi, Catholic and Jewish Kabbalah traditions. Scholars point out that accurate historical or manuscript evidence for lyrics and biographies of Hindu saint-poets is meager at best. Yet, they are fondly remembered in their regions as saintly figures who sang their songs of *bhakti* freely among people outside of formal religious contexts. People from all strata of the society have sung their songs for centuries. These are like popular hymns in other religions of the world such as "Amazing Grace." Set in regionally popular melodies and transmitted through performance, the songs of saint-poets can be heard today in diverse contexts – in devotional gatherings, in voices of women sweeping their front yards or a solitary reaper in a farm, on regional radio-stations, in school prayers, in non-religious concerts, and in temples. Using language of common people in their songs, some saint-poets, as Christian Novetzke has shown, played key roles in getting their vernaculars the status of literary languages that began to be used on public and formal platforms.

Who were these saint-poets? And where do they fit in the basics of Hinduism? The traditions of saint-poets emerged in the centuries following the development of the Puranic mythology when the path of *bhakti* gained greater popularity among large sections of the society over the paths of *jnān* and *karma*. The earliest known traditions of this type, where the poet's subjectivity as a devotee is at the core, arose in the Tamil region of South India between the sixth and the tenth centuries. Here, two distinct lineages of saint-poets developed – one dedicated to Shiva (*nāyanārs*) and the other to Vishnu (*ālvārs*). The saint-poets were men and women who came from a range of social backgrounds including Brahmins at one end of the caste hierarchy and Dalits at the other. Their songs provided foundational texts for two major sects dedicated to Shiva and Vishnu. In these sects, the songs came to have Veda-like status as indicated by the apt title – *The Vernacular Veda* – of Vasudha Narayanan's book on the tradition around the songs of the *ālvārs*. Within the next three centuries a major group of Shiva devotee poets composed lyrics called *vacana*s in Kannada, forming a classic corpus in the language. These poems too are key texts within another Shaiva tradition – Veerashaivism. Such traditions of *bhakti* around songs attributed to saint-poets and legends about them arose in many parts of the subcontinent in the subsequent centuries until the eighteenth. Some of them became associated with different religious sects, while many became greatly popular outside of sectarian contexts too. All of them offered important regional channels for expressing *bhakti*. Even though the traditions in various regions were quite diverse in their orientations and did not have historical links, they overlapped in themes and some core imagery. For example, themes such as Krishna's childhood among cowherds, Rama's compassion, and the glory of the mother goddess are popular in several vernacular *bhakti* songs. Because of their shared aspects, the traditions have often been collectively termed the "*bhakti* movement." But this nomenclature is now questioned by scholars because of the absence of an established historical link among them.

A term frequently associated with singing devotional songs (*bhajans*) composed by saint-poets in several regions of north India is *bhakti-rasa*, which connotes the blissful nectar-like experience of devotion. The term links *bhakti* to *rasa* or "aesthetic delight" (lit. "juice" or "nectar"), a key concept in Indian aesthetics. It conveys the cultural stance that the experience of devotion – especially when evoked through channels like poetry, music, dance, or drama – is akin to aesthetic delight, which leads the enjoyer to forget about worldly concerns for the duration of performance. When absorbed in singing or listening to a *bhajan*, one experiences freedom from one's self-centered desires and the bliss of being close to the divine. This experience is *bhakti-rasa*. Many people believe that singing *bhajans* regularly gradually makes this experience a permanent aspect of consciousness. For this reason, *bhajans* of saint-poets dedicated to Shiva, Krishna, Rama, or the goddess are a part of daily religious practice of many individuals. They are also sung in gatherings, where they become a basis of community building and "sharing," another important connotation of *bhakti*.

How do the songs and hagiographies of saint-poets relate to the Sanskrit texts considered earlier? As an Indian literary scholar suggests, saint-poets were like retailers through whom the spiritual concepts and narratives contained in Sanskrit Vedas, Upanishads, the epics, and the Puranas were repackaged and reached the populace intertwined with regional devotional practices. The lyrics of the saint-poets are broadly categorized into two distinct groups (especially in north India) – those expressing deep love for a single deity who has an anthropomorphic form and qualities (such as Krishna or the goddess) and those focused on the formless divine within oneself (often referenced with the generic term "Rām") through inner search. Those of the first type are categorized as *saguna bhakti* songs; and often their poets as *bhakta-kavi* (devotee poets). Those of the second are termed *nirguna bhakti* songs and their poets *sant*s (saints). There is, however, considerable overlap between them. A few prominent aspects shared by both currents were: (a) a focus on the power of love, (b) disregard for external markers of religion (sometimes even religious identity), and (c) questioning of caste and gender hierarchies in the matters of devotion/spirituality.

Songs expressing devotion to a deity, belonging to the *saguna* category, generally allude to popular Puranic myths with which people are familiar. But many of them offer fresh interpretations of the narratives and skillfully use regional poetic elements, making them classics in their own right, as John Stratton Hawley's fine study of poet Surdas's Krishna *bhakti* lyrics has shown. Here, let us look at a few examples from the lyrics of Gujarat's prominent saint-poet Narasinha Mehta (fifteenth century), who composed *bhajan*s in Gujarati devoted to Krishna. As seen before, the Puranic narratives about Krishna's childhood in the village of Gokul near the Vrindavan forest among cowherds (considered low caste), and his bonds of love with them have been extremely popular. Narasinha's songs (translation mine) question the low status of cowherds in the caste hierarchy. In a popular song describing the child Krishna taking baby steps in his foster parents Nanda and Yashoda's front yard Narasinha says:

> How beautiful Hari (Krishna) looks with his anklets ringing sweetly!
> Blessed are the cowherds!
> What [is to be gained] from being high caste?

In another song putting love of cowherds above mediation of the yogis, he says:

> The one unfathomable through philosophies,
> and refusing to appear in a yogis' meditation,
> that dear one churns the curds in Nanda's house,
> and grazes cows in Vrindavan.

In a song about cowherd women (*gopīs*) complaining to Yashoda about Krishna's naughtiness, they use a Gujarati word of endearment, *nānaḍiyo* ("the little one"). The diminutive highlights their love, giving these "low caste" women a right to chide the earthly incarnation of mighty Vishnu. In yet another song, a *gopī* loved by adolescent Krishna is grateful for being born a woman, a fate generally undesirable in a patriarchal setting:

> *What was my good merit that I was born a woman?*
> *Krishna pleads with me with such meekness.*

Such lines in Narasinha's songs closely parallel verses of the sixteenth-century Jewish mystic Mordecai Dato who made a strong case for women's role in salvation through the figure of Esther in his vernacular Italian poetry. Narasinha's songs subvert the hierarchies of caste and gender as prescribed by orthodoxy and stress their irrelevance on the path of love (*bhakti*). In private and communal performances, they can lead the participants to imaginatively identify with cowherd women and men, and not kings or priests. Such songs found in diverse languages of the subcontinent allow people in various strata of the society to feel validated as devotees. Similar songs of saint-poets expressing devotion to Rama, Shiva, and the goddess can also be heard widely. These too reflect disregard for social hierarchies.

Saint-poets who focus on inner-search, called *sants*, draw concepts and vocabulary from diverse contemplative and meditative traditions of the subcontinent including Upanishadic, Buddhist, Jain, and at times Sufi thought as well as other indigenous mystical currents. They may allude to Puranic myths; but their focus is not the narrative. Their *nirguṇa bhakti* songs either try to draw a roadmap of inner journey through metaphors or exhort the listener to undertake it forsaking external religious practices such as rituals. *Sants* are even more sharply critical of caste hierarchies and belief in ritual purity than *bhakta-kavis* and are equally popular in Hindu communities. One of the most well-known and popular saint-poet of this type is Kabir (ca fifteenth century), who lived in the holy city of Banaras, grew up in a Muslim weaver family, but is known to have had a Hindu spiritual mentor. Kabir himself also had both

Hindu and Muslim disciples, but he did not identify as either. He sang about the divine within all hearts whom he called Rām. Two couplets in Hindi attributed to Kabir give a glimpse into the world of *nirguṇa bhakti* lyrics:

If you call me Hindu, I am not that; nor am I a Mulism
There is only the body made of five elements;
in it, the mysterious one plays.
****
Just as fragrance is within a flower, and reflection within a mirror,
the divine resides within your being, interminably.

In their focus on knowledge rather than ritual and references to the Ultimate as the inner essence of everything (including human heart), Kabir's vernacular songs parallel the Upanishadic thought. They also parallel some profound concepts like "emptiness" found in Buddhist philosophy. Yet these songs do not draw directly or exclusively from elite metaphysical thought. They are rooted in indigenous spiritual ethos in which diverse currents – including philosophical thought of the elite and folk mystical insights – have been getting woven seamlessly with one another for centuries. It is not uncommon to hear people from various strata of the society effortlessly articulating their indifference to worldly success and their supreme confidence in inner Rām using everyday language. Their casual manner indicates that their lives are grounded in the worldview. Songs of popular saint-poets like Kabir are exquisite expressions of that worldview and have nurtured it for generations. Indeed, one of the most profound articulations of what spiritual journey involves I have ever heard was from a Dalit rikshaw (three-wheel cab) driver on a ride from one end of a city to another. He referred to Kabir a few times.

As vernacular *bhakti* currents developed, along with high-caste men, two groups that were earlier not heard, found authentic religious voices. There were several women among regional saint-poets. Their songs integrate several feminine concerns and aspirations with *bhakti* and use imagery from women's everyday life. Some of them – like Mira of Rajasthan, Akka Mahadevi of Karnataka, and Lalla of Kashmir – are celebrated as iconic figures in their own region, widely in the subcontinent, and even internationally. Translations of their songs are found in several languages of the world. There were also equally celebrated lower-caste and Dalit saint-poets – like Ravidas of Banaras and Chokhamela of Maharashtra. In their songs, they allude to the humiliation caused by caste discrimination in the society; but seek refuge in divine grace. Along with devotion, songs of these poets express pride in their devotional identities despite being discriminated against as low-caste and remind recurrently that social hierarchies have no meaning for the divine. Their songs form the core of religious lives of their communities and are also heard in gatherings of "high-caste" devotees.

Legends about saint-poets' lives, which developed in the centuries following their lifetimes, are also heard in all the diverse contexts in which their songs are heard. These reinforce the devotional and moral messages conveyed in the songs by portraying the saint-poets as exemplifying those messages. Narasinha's message about disregarding caste hierarchies is reinforced through narratives about his close bonds with "untouchables." Woman saint Mira sang ecstatically about her loving surrender to Krishna and indifference to her prescribed role as a princess. Her messages are supported by narratives recounting her unshaken faith and her miraculous rescues from attempts on her life by her royal in-laws with Krishna's intervention. The figures of the saint-poets are popular not only because they are inspiring, but also because as men and women in real historical communities, they are more easily relatable for people than devotees found in the Puranic myths who belong to a remote past. Saint-poets have therefore been paradigms of *bhakti* whose memory is kept alive by people in a variety of ways. In the integral links between songs and narratives, the Hindu saint-poet traditions have parallels in other South Asian traditions such as Sikhism and popular Islam/Sufism.

The Warkaris we met in the Introduction take a long yearly pilgrimage on foot singing songs and recalling lives of the saint-poets of their region, Maharashtra. Chaitrali, Rukma's daughter, is teaching poor children a dance using a Hindi song of Surdas, a famous saint-poet from north India. And Chaitrali's friend Arthi performed a classical dance based on songs of the ninth-century woman saint Andal from Tamil Nadu in the annual cultural show of her college in Pune. In modern times, both the songs and the narratives have overflowed from the religious to popular culture (often non-religious) contexts. Saint-poets figure prominently in literary histories, plays, television dramas, and films. Their traditions have indeed been some of the most significant mediators between pan-Indian Sanskritic and popular regional Hindu traditions for centuries. They also open vistas for interfaith dialogues on many occasions.

NARRATIVE PERFORMANCES

In addition to the regional versions of Sanskrit classics and saint-poets' lyrics, numerous other ways of reinterpreting and retelling epic and Puranic narratives have prevailed in regional languages of India for centuries. The most informal narration is enjoyed by children. In the absence of institutions for formal religious education, most Hindu children hear them from their grandparents or elders at home in a piecemeal manner – one day the Ganesha story, another day about Krishna's childhood, and so on. They hear these stories like any other, sometimes while dining, sometimes at bedtime. The lessons they may draw from a Ganesha story may be of respecting parents, the one from a Krishna story may be caring for animals. Other religious meanings of the narratives become clearer to children as they grow.

Narration of stories with exegesis in a structured manner is often heard in public places. Narrators called *kathākār*s who present stories from sacred texts – especially of the *Rāmāyaṇa* and the *Bhāgavata* Purana (Krishna stories) – with commentaries in regional languages have been very popular in all parts of India and even internationally. A *kathā* (retelling) event is generally weeklong with several hours of narration each day. The exegesis in vernacular makes ancient stories relatable in present times. The *kathākār*s are generally great scholars of their texts; but they often intersperse narration with devotional singing, enactment of key episodes, and contemporary stories that exemplify the teaching of a specific narrative.

Another type of retelling of sacred stories occurs through recitation of long narrative poems in regional languages. Written by well-known poets, these poems set the narratives in contexts relatable for regional audiences. Until recently, traveling bards moved from village to village reciting/singing them in open areas at night and were sponsored by local communities. The bards called *mān-bhaṭṭs*, for example, followed such a tradition in Gujarat for centuries. A popular poet in the narrative genre named Premanand presented Puranic narratives almost as if they were taking place in the Gujarat of his time with its landscapes, costumes, foods, and even humor. The recitation of such poems offered both religious education and entertainment. One can also find itinerant performers of folk narrative poems about local deities who are seen as partial or full manifestations of great pan-Indian divinities. Performers from the Nayak Bhil community of the Rajasthan region, for example, musically retell the story of their deity Pabuji, identified as an incarnation of Rama's brother Lakshman in the *Ramayana*. Generally, a woman and a man take turns in singing parts of the story to the accompaniment of a folk instrument called *rāvaṇhatha* and with the backdrop of a wide narrative painting. Another community from the same region, the *jogīs*, are also known for their musical narration. They generally perform in a group in open spaces. But one may also find a *jogī* singer on the street and invite him for a short performance in one's house, which can be enchanting. Years ago, a singer I invited to my apartment in Ahmedabad, moved all present to tears with his narration of deification of a woman of his village, now identified as a manifestation of Shiva's wife Parvati. All these genres of narration make the ancient narratives easily relatable for people in different locales in reconfigured forms. But in these, the listeners are somewhat passive.

Narration of epic and Puranic tales with more active roles for all participants is often found in long folk songs of several communities living close to forests, often classified as tribes that are outside of the caste system. These communities may or may not self-identify as Hindu but have significant overlap in religious vocabulary, narratives, festivals, and practices. They are called the *ādivasīs* or "the first residentss (of the land)," presumably before the arrival of the Sanskrit-speaking Aryans. During major festivals, members of many such communities perform dance or dance-dramas to long folk songs with epic or Puranic narratives. In my childhood, some of the most enjoyable parts of the nine-nights festival of the goddess were performances of traveling troupes of a *rānī-paraj* ("forest people") community named "Dubla" of western India who danced while singing songs in unison. In their songs, Puranic stories were told with reinterpretations in which the roles of tribal deities, heroes, and animals were greatly highlighted in comparison to the deeds of the heroes of the Sanskrit texts. In another example, in songs of Gonds of central India, a she elephant confronts Shiva (identified as Bara Dev) for cutting her child's head as a replacement for Ganesha's and successfully gets a boon for him. Such performances, fondly watched by others living around them, reinforce that Hindu sacred narratives have multiple valid interpretations. Importantly, they offer a window into the exchanges between Sanskrit-based and non-Sanskritic traditions that have shaped the Hindu worlds.

FOLK THEATER

Just as diverse as other narrative forms are regional theaters of India, some of which have developed into sophisticated art forms with dance and drama intricately intertwined. Most of these forms developed in the latter half of the second millennium. Many are not exclusively religious; but often encompass religious themes and narration. These include *Ramlīlā* (Rama's play) of north India, *Kathakali* (story performance) of Kerala, *Bhavāi* (emotion for the mother goddess) of Gujarat, *Yakshagana* (play of spirits) of Karanataka, *Jātra* (journey) of Bengal and Orissa, *Ankiya Naat* (one-act plays on Krishna) of Assam, *Dasāvatar* (ten incarnations) from Konkan, *Kāttī-pyākha* (Kartik dance) of Nepal, and the list goes on. *Ramlīlā* is also performed in many countries like Fiji where people from north India have migrated. In these plays, mythic and epic narratives are reinterpreted in a variety of ways and are often mixed with humor and social satire that address contemporary issues. The distinction between the purely religious and the secular is blurred in these plays, which have aspects of both ritual and entertainment. Traditionally, folk theater performances are meant for small local audiences with sponsorship and donations from the wealthy among them. Some of these are based on plays by well-known writers; and some on scripts written by folk authors. In many, the performers come from diverse caste backgrounds and the plays contain sharp critiques of caste hierarchies. But some are strictly regulated by high-caste performers and may not allow low-caste audiences. The performances are generally on temporary stages. These regional theaters can be compared to Mystery and Morality plays of medieval Europe, which dramatized miracles from the Old and the New Testaments and had their origins in the church; but gradually became popular vernacular theater forms. Unlike their European counterparts, however, these regional theaters have continued to survive, gradually evolving into cherished folk-art forms.

WOMEN'S TEXTS

The texts we have discussed above are freely accessible to both men and women. But there are also vernacular texts specifically used by women, found in diverse regions of India and Nepal. Use of both these types of texts by women forms an important "basic" of Hinduism because it is the entry-point for most Hindu children's religious education. In the absence of formal institutions like Christian Sunday schools or Muslim *madrassa*s in the traditional Hindu context, religious lessons for a child begin generally with what they hear from their mothers, grandmothers, or other close female relatives. The melodies of saint-poets' and festival songs as well as narration of stories by their mothers are integrally woven with other sounds of the kitchen, aromas of special foods, loving gestures, and warmth of caressing hands of mothers/aunts get linked to the understanding of religion for the children.

Chaitrali and Ravi, Rukma's children whom we met in the introduction, have heard their mother sing, or hum, her favorite Marathi *bhajan* (called *abhang* in the language) – *rhuṇu jhuṇu ruṇu jhuṇu re bhramara* (o buzzing black bee) – as long as they can remember. She can be heard singing it softly in the kitchen or in a full-throated manner when she thinks she is alone. This popular song, by aforementioned saint-poet Jnaneshwar, addresses the mind as a restless buzzing bee. It has been discussed in literary circles for centuries. But for Chaitrali and Ravi, it is associated with their mother's happiest moments and taste of *poli* (flat bread) and *varan* (lentil soup) that she could be making for them while singing. My own earliest memory of learning anything about "religion" is linked to saint-poet Mira's song about her resolve to leave her palace and follow a life of devotion. My mother sang it regularly as she tucked us to bed. The image of a princess escaping in the darkness of night to sing and dance in *bhakti* among commoners is etched in my mind and linked with the melody of her song. Women are thus important transmitters of religious knowledge in Hindu communities. The texts specifically used by them in homes, extended families, and close-knit communities therefore form a major core of the tradition.

Among many genres of vernacular texts for women, three are widespread: (a) narratives for *vrata* (vow or votive) rites, (b) folk and festival songs, and (c) songs related to life cycle rituals. In all three, women are represented as active religious agents. Many texts make clear references to women as manifesting the creative energy of the universe – *śakti*, allowing them to feel empowered in the moment. A *vrata* is a ritual observed on a designated day or over a period, generally with some type of fasting, prayer, and at times pilgrimage. Its roots can be traced back to the Vedas where several references to it are found. Most widely performed *vrata*s today, however, are related to Puranic or regional deities (often goddesses). Narratives about these deities are retold during *vrata* performances in regional languages. While *vrata*s may be undertaken by men, they are most frequently performed by women. Many narratives for *vrata*s have a female votary at the center. The woman in the story successfully performs a strict fast or fulfills a difficult vow, paralleling an ascetic practice. As a reward, she is blessed by a deity with a long life of her husband, health of her children, or well-being of her family. A *vrata* story is generally retold in a group or read from inexpensive printed booklets, with an expectation that the narrator/reader and listeners too will receive blessings similar to the ones received by the votary in the narrative.

To look at just a few examples, the narrative retold during a widely observed *vrata* in many parts of India – *vaṭa-savitri* – is about Savitri, who gets the life of her husband back from the deity of death, Yama. Found in the *Mahabharata*, the narrative stresses Savitri's dedication to her husband and the strength of her resolve in standing up to Yama. A similar narrative is told about a woman named Karva in north India, where women perform the *vrata* of Karva Chauth for their husbands' long lives with a strict daylong fast. Often, the story of a queen who was able to revive her husband by performing this *vrata* is told along with that of Karva. In Nepal's Kathmandu valley a monthlong *vrata* of goddess Svasthani is popular. In its narrative, goddess Svasthani helps Shiva's first wife Sati to overcome grief when her husband is insulted by her father. The goddess also advises Sati to get reborn as Parvati and win Shiva over again. Jessica V. Birkenholtz's study of this text indicates that women retell this story praying for a good life for their husbands and young unmarried women for a good husband.

The *vrata* narratives have paradoxical implications for women. On the one hand, they offer women a sense of agency as contributing significantly to the family's material and spiritual well-being, which is appreciated by the family. On the other hand, unlike ascetic practices described in classical texts that are believed to lead to a person's spiritual advancement, the fasts and strenuous religious pursuits of women in many of these narratives are meant to serve others, not themselves. While some women are uncomfortable with *vrata* narratives for this reason, most of those who regularly perform them focus on the agency aspect. In recent years, progressive men have begun to fast on the day of Karwa Chauth for their wives' long lives.

The second genre of women's sacred texts is festival songs and folk songs with religious themes. While the *vrata* stories often reinforce patriarchal gender norms, in these songs women's voices are free, assertive, and often subversive. Many songs use well-known sacred narratives as the basis, but give womanist interpretations. Some express self-perceptions of women as confident religious and social agents influencing their own and others' lives. Songs may be associated with specific festivals; or they may be sung at any time while doing household chores or in informal gatherings. The idiom, metaphors and images, and the aspirations have a feminine touch. Let us look at a few examples from various regions. Songs related to the *Ramayana* sung by women of various castes in Andhra

Pradesh are finely discussed by Velachuru Rao. Among these, some songs of Brahmin women tell the narrative from Sita's perspective. Here, Sita is not openly defiant but uses every opportunity to free herself from the pressure of Rama's expectations. She is helped by her female relatives and even Ravana's sister, indicating a collective aspiration for freedom from patriarchal norms among women. In a song of women from "lower" castes, Sita does not request Rama to get her the golden deer (which led to her abduction in the original story), she asks for his bow and arrow so that she can hunt it herself. In the Himalayan region near Nandadevi, women's songs address Shiva's consort Parvati (whose name means "of the mountain") as their daughter and invite her to her natal home for festivals.

In Gujarat, during the festival of the goddess lasting nine nights, Navaratri, women sing songs called *garbā* in which they invite her to dance with them as a friend. The great goddess who destroyed demons to protect the world is praised as both the divine mother and a friend dancing with women in open spaces at night for hours singing *garbā* songs. Treating the goddess as a friend, they tell her about their wishes and troubles. Sometimes, they make fun of their husbands or in-laws, taking advantage of being in the company of the goddess. Here are a few lines from such a Gujarati song:

> I had gone to dance (in garbā) in the bright night, and came home tired.
> "Mother-in-law, give me something to eat." (I said)
> Mother-in-law gave me porridge with one drop of oil.
> (then I turned to my mother)
> "Mother dear, give me something to eat"
> Mother gave me a sweet with lots of butter.

Having danced with the goddess, the woman not only feels confident enough to order the mother-in-law, but she also feels comfortable to point out her (mother-in-law's) miserliness in making a porridge with one drop of oil, which compares poorly with the sweet with lots of butter offered by the mother. As we can see, in these songs the divine beings of the Hindu pantheon do not remain distant transcendent beings only to be revered; but appear as loving friends and almost as family members in whom the singing women can confide and whose support they can seek. Even with several aspects of traditional religious life disappearing from the contemporary world, many of these songs remain popular and circulate in markets, recorded in voices of major artists.

If festival songs bring the divine beings into women's worlds, the third major genre of vernacular texts of women, elevate the status of rite-of-passage ceremonies like birth and weddings by associating them with divine beings. On arrival of a baby (traditionally a baby boy, but now also a baby girl), songs related to Krishna's arrival to his foster parents' home and happiness of cowherds are sung. Wedding songs are replete with references to festivities during Rama and Sita's wedding, Krishna's love with Radha, and Shiva and Parvati's conjugal happiness. A wedding song from Gujarat, for example, depicts the joy of the human couple as they fall in love through allusion to the first encounter of Rama and Sita:

> (In the garden)
> Rama hit Sita with a ball made of flowers.
> Sita took her revenge by hitting him with the stick of a clove.

Until the late twentieth century, songs sung by female relatives made the festivities of any life-cycle ceremony come alive and had a central role to play in them. But they are now being replaced by popular film songs or recorded wedding songs. While Hindu women have made strides in professional fields in recent times, in this area, their voices have receded in significance.

THE PLACE OF VERNACULAR SACRED TEXTS IN THE HINDU WORLDS

As the above survey shows, vernacular texts in popular genres shape the religious imagination of a large majority of Hindus and are used much more extensively than the ancient Sanskrit texts, which have been largely inaccessible to the masses. The inaccessibility of elite texts, however, has not resulted in deprivation of active religious life for average Hindus since Hinduism is not centered on one book or canonized scriptures. In the regional texts preserved in people's voices and embodied performances, ancient narratives get reinterpreted and expanded, often in a subversive manner. In some, even choices of characters with divine status are questioned; and in some higher status is given to regionally wor-shipped deities. Regional texts also highlight local customs and rites-of-passage specific to the region. They generally extol the path of *bhakti*; but many also grapple with issues of *dharma* or moral duty from different angles. People who do not have religious authority still have authentic religious experience through them. Because of the extent to which they inform and nurture religious lives of a large majority of Hindus, they are not of secondary importance; they are mainstream Hindu compositions along with (or perhaps even more than) the foundational and formative San-skrit texts.

The significance of the vernacular texts in the lives of lay Hin-dus is evident. But their popularity is also tapped into for business, social, and political purposes. Several singers from communities considered "low-caste" follow religious paths named after saint-poet Kabir, one of the fiercest critics of caste, and sing his songs both as spiritual practice and articulation of pride in their identity. Linda Hess gives a rich account of such singing events in her book *Bodies of Song*. Communities following the Dalit saint-poet Ravi-das have also established institutions in his name to reclaim their dignity and their contribution to India's cultural history. But at times, genres of *bhakti* are also recreated for nationalist and/or political purposes as Anna Schultz has shown in her work on a genre of Marathi devotional performance. In my work on Gujarati Hindu women's songs and dance worshipping the goddess, *garbā*, I have discussed how they have been turned into profitable business in contemporary times. Yet, all these usages and/or manipulations are possible because performative regional texts have a tremendous hold over people. Their nonreligious uses reinforce their signifi-cance as a sustaining force of Hindu religious life. Average Hindus highly value the religious agency and authenticity these texts offer to them without priestly intervention. But this does not mean that they reject Sanskrit sources. People engage with Sanskrit texts (even if it involves chanting only a few verses) when they find it appropriate, with or without a guide. Hindu religious life is gener-ally regulated by need and preferences of individuals in which the dynamics of Sanskrit and vernacular texts are intricately interwoven.

Table 3.1 summarizes the significance of various vernacular sacred texts genres and gives an indication of the layered nature of religious agency they offer to Hindus outside of the priestly circle.

Table 3.1 Performative Vernacular Texts

Genre	Performers/participants	Significance
Epics in vernacular and commentary on BG	Neighborhood or family groups and professional narrators (generally upper caste)	Accessibility, reinterpretation of original texts with different foci
Songs of saint-poets	Individuals or groups of all castes in informal *bhakti* routines; professional public performers	Expression of *bhakti* in people's voice with reinterpretation of classical texts; reaffirmation of regional culture; challenge to caste hierarchies
Kathā (narration) of epic and Puranas	Professional *kathākārs* with extensive training; large audiences	Accessible exegesis interpretation with focus on contemporary relevance
Folk epics	Hereditary public performers/singers	Honoring of regional deities (as manifestations of Puranic deities) and value system
Long narrative poems (folk or *ādivāsī*)	Community members at festivals	Celebration of local/tribal deities and heroes (at times, as more important than the Puranic ones)
Folk theater	Community members (in some with extensive training and caste bars)	Often addressing contemporary sociopolitical issues with humor; blurring the boundaries between the sacred and the secular
Women's texts – *vrata* narratives, songs for festival and ceremonies	Groups of women	Somewhat paradoxical – articulation of women's religious agency, but often reinforcing patriarchal expectations

FURTHER EXPLORATION SUGGESTIONS

Ch-02: Sanskriti. "Indian Traditional Theater Form." Swayam Prabha, Information and Library Network. Government of India. Accessed July 9, 2022. https://www.youtube.com/c/Ch02SANSKRITIArts HistoryPhilosophy/search.

Hawley, John Stratton, and Mark Juergensmeyer. 2008. *Songs of the Saints of India.* New Delhi: Oxford University Press.

Meena, Madan. 2018. "Jogi Community of Rajasthan and *Raja Bharthari-ki-Katha.*" Sahapedia online Encyclopedia of Indian Culture. Accessed July 9, 2022. https://www.sahapedia.org/jogi-community-of-rajasthan-and-raja-bharthari-ki-katha.

Pintchman, Tracy. 2007. *Women's Lives, Women's Rituals in the Hindu Tradition.* Oxford: Oxford University Press.

Raheja, Gloria Goodwin, and Ann Grodzins Gold. 1994. *Listen to the Heron's Words: Reimagining Gender and Kinship in North India.* Berkeley, CA: University of California Press.

Shukla-Bhatt, Neelima. 2014. *Narasinha Mehta of Gujarat: A Legacy of Bhakti in Songs and Stories.* New York, NY: Oxford University Press.

Singh, Karan. 2019. *Folk Theaters of North India: Contestation, Amalgamation and Transference.* Milton: Taylor & Francis Group.

Zelliot, Eleanor, and Rohini Mokashi-Punekar. 2005. *Untouchable Saints: An Indian Phenomenon.* New Delhi: Manohar.

4

SOCIAL ORGANIZATION AND
GOALS FOR INDIVIDUAL LIFE

A major pillar of a religious culture is the guidelines it offers to individuals regarding appropriate goals for life and social responsibility. In this chapter, we will consider that pillar of Hinduism. We will review the enduring influence of some norms prescribed by ancient *dharma* texts on social and individual life within Hindu communities. We will also look at the roles of vernacular texts that influence moral values and caste councils (*panchāyats*) that regulate ethical and social behavior of people in communities locally. These preclude a verbatim following of the injunctions of the *dharma* texts by every Hindu, as is sometimes assumed. Like all other aspects of Hinduism, the sources for guidance for a good life and social responsibility are layered. They contain prescriptions, at times stating dire consequences for their disregard; but they are not commandments. In the absence of a centralized religious institution with judicial authority, in ancient and medieval times, the punitive measures for disregard of prescribed injunctions were either taken up by royal courts or imposed by the society through various ways of exclusion. In modern times, social exclusion has been the main form of disciplinary measures, but it is fast losing its impactfulness with increasing stress on individual choice. Further, there is no concept of heresy or blasphemy in Hinduism by which an adherent

DOI: 10.4324/9781315303352-5

can be judged. In this chapter, reviewing some sources of guidance, we will explore: (a) the organization of Hindu society in a hereditary and hierarchical system of group identity, widely termed "caste," (b) status of roles for women, and (c) goals for individual life. We begin with social organization rather than individual life goals since in some ways the latter are embedded in the former.

ORGANIZATION OF SOCIETY – "CASTE"

In previous chapters, we have seen references to the organization of the Hindu society into occupation related hereditary and hierarchically ordered groups – castes –that has had clearly discriminatory implications. This is one of the aspects of Hinduism that have received the most attention in public discourses around the world. Some people view caste not simply as an aspect of Hinduism but rather as synonymous with it. Caste therefore deserves close attention. The term "caste" is not indigenous, of course. It is a term originally used by the Spanish in the early sixteenth century to denote "race" or "tribe." It was employed by the Portuguese to refer to the various endogamous communities they encountered when they established their colonies in India the sixteenth century onward. The term later came to be used globally to refer to the Hindu social organization. Yet the term conflates two interrelated Indian terms, *varṇa* and *jāti*. *Varṇa* refers to a broad categorization of the society into four groups – priests (Brahmins), warriors and kings (Kshatriyas), merchants and craftsmen (Vaishyas), and servants (Shudras) – hierarchically ordered in terms of their religious status based on the criterion of ritual purity, whereas *jāti* denotes an endogamous community traditionally associated with a specific hereditary occupation and is self-governed in many ways. When a person mentions her/his caste, the reference is generally to their *jāti*. The term *varṇa* is hardly ever used in everyday conversations.

There are literally hundreds of *jāti*s in each part of India. Some *jāti*s are found widely, while some are distinctive to each region, partly based on geography. For example, fishing communities are naturally found in coastal regions and not in landlocked ones. Each *jāti* loosely aligns with a *varṇa*. But this alignment is not permanently fixed. It varies region to region and also in different historical contexts. In each context, as sociologist M.N. Srinivas has discussed, some *jāti*s that are numerically strong acquire political and/or economic power also gain dominance over others whether they have high religious status or not. This may lead a *jāti* to slide from one *varṇa* to another and on the scale of hierarchy. Only the priestly *varṇa* has remained relatively stable since ancient times in terms of *jāti*s belonging to it. It is important to note here that the role of a "priest" in Hinduism differs strikingly from the one found in other traditions. A Hindu priest does not preach in a temple or function as a spiritual guide; nor does he have jurisdiction over people's religious life. A priest in Hinduism is fundamentally a ritual specialist who officiates ceremonies for families, communities, or in temples closely following Vedic or other sacred texts. A learned priest may also train other priests in scriptures and ritual performance. He has a high status but less authority over community and individual lives than priests in some other traditions. It is helpful to keep this in view in understanding the working of the caste system. Since caste is a distinct social system with a truly long history, some questions that arise about it are: How did this system originate? What were its implications at the time? How has it worked over the centuries and what is its state now? Exploring these questions with some scholarly insights can help us understand this aspect of Hinduism to an extent. A comprehensive examination of this extremely complex and over two millennia old system is not possible here.

DEVELOPMENT OF THE CASTE (VARṆA AND JĀTI) SYSTEM

It is generally accepted by scholars that Aryans who migrated to India already had a tripartite social system, flexibly divided into priests, warriors, and commoners. The servants were added later. As mentioned in Chapter 2, the textual origins of the caste system are often traced to a verse in RV 10.90, which describes how the creation emerged when the Supreme Man sacrificed Himself. The hymn presents everything in the universe – birds, animals, days, planets, and the Vedas – as originating from a singular divine source. The hymn reflects the almost obsessive tendency of ancient Indian thinkers to classify things, elements, natural products, and people with what they considered a universally applicable order, as Brian K. Smith has observed. One verse in it states that the four *varna*s came out of His mouth, arms, thighs, and feet. Hierarchy (related to the highest to the lowest parts of the divine body) is implicit in this verse; but there is no mention of heredity. There have been extensive debates about the dating of the hymn since the nineteenth century. Contemporary scholars generally agree that it was a later addition to *Rig* Veda (RV), perhaps to claim Vedic authority for hierarchy once it became established. In the early Vedic era, the *varna* hierarchy prevailed in an embryonic form.

Clear references to the four *varna*s are found in later Vedic texts and the *Gita* (BG). In these, the sense of hierarchy is stronger – with Brahmins placed at the top. But these texts are not specifically concerned about systematically organizing society. Prescriptions for social hierarchy with discrimination and stratified *varna–jāti* boundaries are generally associated with *dharma* treatises (fourth-century BCE–fourth-century CE, discussed earlier as formative texts). Of these the *Manu Dharmaśāstra* is considered prominent and has also received most attention in academic and public discourses. We will therefore mainly refer to it here. Some scholars think that *jāti* was likely an indigenous non-Aryan system that became integrated with the *varna* system in the social organization as described in *dharma* texts. Following Louise Dumont's influential work *Homo Hierarchicus* (1966), many scholars agreed that the structures of hierarchy as prescribed by these texts were based on notions of inherent purity and pollution of human groups among whom Brahmins were seen as the purest and were expected to follow stringent rules of behavior for it. Each *varna* lower on the ladder was seen as relatively less pure in a graded manner and those outside of all *varna*s as polluted. At the same time, Dumont observed that higher rank in this schema did not mean greater power or wealth. A similar observation made by Brian K. Smith is that it is possible that throughout history the ceremonially high status of Brahmins was not indicative of their social power.

More recently, Sanskrit scholar Patrick Olivelle (1998) has made two observations based on a close linguistic analysis of *dharma* texts.

First, the *dharma* treatises like Manu's were not so concerned with inherent purity as they were with establishing processes for purifying a person's state. They can be read as manuals for purification. Manu's text, with its focus on the behavior of a Brahmin man, for example, has numerous verses specifying actions or situations that lead to his fall (being blemished) and ways to return to a purified state. Olivelle's second observation is that the *dharma* texts did not create social structures but rather reinforced the existing ones with an authoritative tone.

In Chapter 10 of Manu's treatise there is a section on the implications of marriages in which the husband and wife belong to different *varṇa*s. The children of several types of mixed marriages are assigned no position in the ārya society even as Shudras. They are referenced as so impure that their touch is polluting. Harsh and humiliating conditions such as living outside of a village and eating in broken dishes are prescribed for them. For occupations, demeaning tasks such as cleaning streets and picking up dead animals are specified for them. But was Manu creating new conditions? This section uses expressions like "established" (*iti sthiti*) or "remembered" (*smṛta*), indicating their prior prevalence. As discussed by Y. Krishnan, references to castes in Buddhist texts of this period corroborate that such hierarchies had become a social reality by this time. The *dharma* texts like Manu's reinforced it using strong religious terms. At the same time, as mentioned in Chapter 1, *dharma*, as it appears in these treatises, is context-sensitive. Hindus often say that *dharma* has to be modified according to *des-kāl* (locale and time) when they need to deviate from the norms because of the context. Further, a few verses in *dharma* treatises suggest that their writers were not sure about the validity of the norms they were prescribing. The same chapter of Manu's treatise that prescribes harsh norms for outcasts contains a verse (10.73) that states that the Creator has declared that the Aryans and non-Aryans who take on one another's behavior are neither equal nor unequal. Two other verses (10.126–127) state that except for the Vedic chanting, Shudras may observe all practices of *dharma*. Even with ambivalence reflected in such verses in *dharma* texts, however, it is certain that discriminatory hierarchical social organization has been a reality in Hindu communities for two millennia.

IMPLICATIONS OF CASTE FOR VARIOUS COMMUNITIES

Among Hindus in India and elsewhere, people belonging to *jāti*s that are clearly aligned to the upper three *varṇa*s, especially Brahmins, have enjoyed high social status, even though not necessarily power and affluence. At regional levels, *jāti*s that have enjoyed political and financial dominance in different historical contexts are the ones that have had greater control over land and means of material production. These vary in regions and may or may not belong to upper castes. All communities have followed endogamy and generally avoided inter-dining. Accepting food from castes higher than one's own, however, is common. *Jāti*s loosely aligned with non-priestly *varṇa*s including Shudra have at times moved on the scale of hierarchy when the nature or significance of their occupations or their material, political or social realities underwent change. Some injunctions found in texts like Manu become irrelevant in contexts when occupations disappear or their status changes.

The *jāti*s that have suffered most discrimination consistently are the ones put outside of the *varṇa* grid and came to get the "untouchable" status. Severe restrictions on their movements in villages and towns have excluded them from decently paying occupations. A large percentage of them have remained landless laborers or followed occupations requiring intense and demeaning labor with meager financial gains. Their exclusion from elite ritual spaces and temples, and their discriminatory treatment in village gatherings have left deep scars of humiliation among them. Members of many such communities now identify themselves as "Dalits" (trampled upon) and rightly demand social justice denied to them for centuries. Several modern Hindu leaders have made efforts to bring about change in this aspect of their society. In independent India, caste discrimination is punishable by law. Universal adult franchise and measures of mandatory affirmative action in education and government employment are put in place. These have resulted in some visible changes in areas such as education and government jobs where a percentage of Dalits have seen socioeconomic success. Yet atrocities to Dalits, especially those locked in labor intensive jobs, are regularly reported, indicating that the problem is far from over.

As seen in earlier chapters, there have, however, always been a few voices since the time of Upanishads that have challenged discriminatory hierarchies of caste. The epics and Puranas too contain narratives that challenge the notion; the regional saint-poets clearly derided caste hierarchies. In contemporary times, a good percentage of upper-caste Hindus acknowledge the social injustice that Dalits have historically suffered in the *varṇa-jāti* system. Many of them engage in some corrective activity. Chaitrali, the young woman of the Kulkarni family whom we first met in the Introduction, teaches festival dances to children in low-caste and Dalit communities in such an effort. Some of my school and college teachers made regular efforts to get financial assistance for students from Dalit communities. Caste hierarchies are recognized as unjust and in the need of erasure by these Hindus. But they do not agree with the view that Hinduism is synonymous with the *varṇa-jāti* system. They view caste as an institution that developed over history rather than as a part of fundamental and unalterable religious teachings of Hinduism. In many ways, caste as a system of organizing society is also prevalent among non-Hindus in South Asia. Several of them continue to follow caste with its salient aspects of heredity and hierarchy even after they convert to other religions.

THE HORIZONTAL DIMENSION OF CASTE AND NARRATIVES OF ORIGIN

With the clearly discriminatory implications of caste, the ostensive question is: What advantage could "lower caste" and Dalit Hindus or non-Hindus in South Asia have seen in following it for so long? An important reason appears to be what one can call "the horizontal dimension of caste," which is seen by members of a community as offering stability. This aspect of caste, which explains its continued existence to an extent (**but certainly does not justify it**), gets often ignored because of its starkly discriminatory vertical axis. What does a caste's "horizontal dimension" mean? In premodern societies, which did not have government or other public institutions offering social care, a caste with its distinctive customs and culture offered its members a sense of belonging and a ready-made support network. Whether high or low on the vertical bar, on the horizontal axis of a caste, i.e., within a community, people could turn to one another for emotional and/or financial support in times of crisis. Even now, it is not uncommon for people to seek funding for education from their caste organizations or wealthier individuals within their community. With the implementation of affirmative action set by the Indian constitution and with their own efforts, several individuals from the lower strata of the society have achieved financial and professional success. Such individuals often serve both as inspiration and sources of financial/professional support for younger generations in their castes. During my undergraduate years, the education of some of my classmates was generously supported by their caste organizations.

In addition to support, the horizontal dimension of caste is also linked to regulating family life and preserving distinctive customs of the community. As mentioned before, to a large extent, *jāti*s are self-governed groups. Since Sanskrit *dharma* treatises were almost exclusively directed toward Brahmins and Kshatriyas and were not even accessible to others, the community life of various castes was not regulated according to them. For each caste, a council of local/regional elders (mostly men), called *panchāyat* in many parts of India, has traditionally established regulations and settled disputes according to the customs of the community. Brahmins have no authority in these areas of community life. The role of caste *panchāyat*s is especially crucial in settling disputes in matters related to marriage, family, and inheritance. In traditional contexts, people generally did not disregard the decisions/verdicts (including fines) made by their caste *panchāyat* because they could be excommunicated and lose community support.

While support mechanisms and the *panchāyat* contribute to internal stability, what helps in positive self-perceptions and interactions in the broader society are mythical narratives that various castes retell about their origins. These are transmitted from generation to generation and have nothing in common with the Vedic hymn to the Supreme Man. Especially interesting are the ones from castes considered lower in hierarchy and Dalit communities. In many myths of Dalits from southern India studied by Robert Deliege, there is a pair of Brahmin brothers, one of whom (often the elder one) makes an inadvertent mistake and gets thrown out from his society. The outcast person and his descendants, however, continue to render crucial services for the society and emerge as morally superior. I heard two such narratives during my fieldwork in Gujarat – one from an old Dalit man and one from a potter. The Dalit man recounted that their progenitor worshipped the earth and kept it clean as a form of worship. Due to the trickery of upper castes, this worship was turned into polluting work and their caste became "untouchable." The potter man said that their community – which makes festival images of deities – was blessed by God to make images that everyone worships. But their work with clay came to have low status. Potters in Gujarat and in many other parts of India identify as Prajapati – descendants of one of the most powerful Vedic deities. Dalit Jogi singers of Rajasthan identify as descendants of Shiva.

It is noteworthy that in most caste narratives, the society pushes people down and not the divine beings, who are, in fact, often presented as endowing the downtrodden communities with important occupational skills. The deities remain beloved among these communities and are worshiped ardently. Many sociologists view such narratives of self-representation as channels for gaining validation within a hierarchical system since none of them explicitly oppose caste. Some see this lack of opposition as reflecting the insidious nature of caste. Yet if we take into consideration the aspects of bonding, support, and community governance discussed above, the draw of caste in the pre-modern era can be understood to an extent. In contemporary times, with other avenues for support being available, caste bonds are slowly losing their relevance. The narratives are not important to the younger generations. Two paradoxical approaches to caste are seen in contemporary India. On the one hand, many advocate the end of caste. On the other, for historically discriminated communities, articulating caste identity offers a platform for solidarity in resistance to injustice. Caste identities also remain important in elections with different communities often seen as forming voting blocs.

WOMEN IN THE HINDU SOCIETY

Having considered caste, now let us turn to gender. Like most traditional societies in the world, the Hindu society has been ostensibly patriarchal since ancient times. It is sometimes said that

Hinduism has a paradoxical view of the feminine with strong god-desses but subordinated women. When we look at the layered cor-pus of its sacred texts and its history of practices, we find a consistent tension between the more liberal and conservative perspectives as is also found in other traditions. Sometimes passages of the same text have contradictory messages. Looking at the tensions in texts and practices helps us understand the status and roles of Hindu women.

Beginning with the earliest phase, in some Vedic texts including the Upanishads, voices of a few women are heard clearly. Vedic rituals also required participation of women. However, they were required only as wives of ritual performers; they were not main performers themselves. In the next phase of Hinduism, in epics, there are a range of female characters, some very strong and able to advise their husbands; whereas some are meek and completely dependent on their male relatives. A few Purana passages give women a place with goddesses on a continuum of the creative energy of the universe, *śakti*. But except for Krishna's companions – cowherd women of Vraj – in the *Bhāgavata Purāna*, there are few memorable strong female characters.

Among Sanskrit texts, the ones that have drawn most attention with regard to gender in public discourses are the *dharma* texts, a majority of which are focused on the behavior of high-caste men and are considered pillars of orthodoxy. These contain only a few passages related to women that instruct men about how to engage with them in ritual and household contexts. Yet, these texts too do not have a uniform approach. There is discernible tension among liberal and conservative passages here too. Some often cited conservative verses from Manu's text (5.147–149, 9.1–2), for example, stress that women should be constantly kept dependent and protected by men in their families – father, brothers, hus-band, and sons – at different stages in life. Another verse (2.67) clearly states that for a woman, serving her husband and taking care of the household are equivalents of the study of the Vedas and performance of the fire sacrifice. At the same time, the text also has verses (3.55–60) in which men are asked emphatically to honor women and keep them happy. They state that only those households prosper in which women are happy. Where they are

unhappy, no ritual gives reward and the family parishes. The section concludes by pronouncing that the households where the
husband is pleased with his wife and the wife with her husband
have everlasting happiness.

The sacred texts apparently provide resources for both conservative and liberal attitudes for women's status and roles. Yet historically, the restrictive passages have been more widely influential.
Women's public roles have been limited and their social status has
not been aligned with the concept of *śakti* except in a few contexts.
Generally, the norm for them has been to dedicate their lives to
their husbands and families. A woman dedicated to her husband is
called *pativratā* and is held in high regard. Within this framework
however, women have consistently negotiated roles and religious
agency for themselves. For example, following the age-old taboo
related to blood, women generally do not perform religious ceremonies in their "polluted" states of menstruation or childbirth. But
many women use their time in these states, especially monthly periods, to pursue hobbies or read sacred texts in vernaculars (because
they are freed from all household duties including cooking).
Similarly, using their traditionally prescribed roles as a platform,
women often undertake rites for the well-being of their families in
which they are independent performers without priestly presence.
They use vernacular texts that we considered in Chapter 3. While
these rites reinforce the patriarchal norms in some ways, they also
provide opportunities for women to bond and create support networks in the absence of men. The mood at their performance is
celebratory with a great deal of laughing and sharing. Therefore,
for a better understanding of the roles and norms for Hindu women,
in addition to ancient texts, considering women's vernacular genres
and dimensions of their actual use is important.

In the area of family finances too, a layered situation prevails.
Since Hindu women's primary sphere has been home and not the
world outside, men have been seen as the breadwinners for their
families. Yet, economists C. Binder and M. Easwaran have shown
that women's work has been central to building the professional
success of their families in traditional Indian societies. Almost all
work for most traditional occupations was done at home with
women as major contributors to it. Acquiring skills in husband's

hereditary occupation was important for women who lived with their in-laws after marriage. Endogamy in the caste system ensured that having grown up in a household with the same occupation as her husband's, the wife had skills in it. An important reason for endogamy, as per these economists, was economic rather than religious. During my family's visits to our ancestral village, I have had opportunities to observe some of these on ground. There, the farmers' wives are adept in farming routines through the year and carpenters' wives in matters related to carpentry. The same is the case in the households of priests and grocers. It is also not uncommon to see women, especially older ones, enjoying command over their families because of their skills in dealing with customers. Women, however, have not been independent owners of property. Since ancient times, their right to property has been through their husbands, though they are well protected in adversity. Even a text like Manu's, considered highly orthodox, stresses that the king must protect the property rights of women in distress, without children, or widowed; and punish as thieves the relatives who try to usurp her assets (8.28–29). Daughters, on the other hand, were given generous gifts at marriage but did not have equal rights over parental property until recently. In contemporary India, with amendments in law after years of activism, Hindu women finally have an equal right to property of their natal families too.

In general, the roles and status of Hindu women have been similar to those in other traditional societies. The situation of upper-caste widows, however, has been more difficult. In extreme and rare cases in history in some regions, a widow climbed the funeral pyre of her husband. Such a woman was called a *satī* (the truthful/ loyal woman) and would later likely be deified by her community. The origins of the practice, also called *satī*, are traced to the sixth century. But its specific origins remain unknown. It is not mentioned in any Vedic or *dharma* texts, some of which like Manu, in fact, mention widow remarriage (Manu 9.175–176). At times during the medieval period, *satī* was voluntarily performed by war-widows as the last resort to escape rape and abduction. In later periods, encouragement/force by the in-laws, who were either too poor to support the woman or greedy for her property, became major factors. Even then, the practice was always rare. During the colonial period, however, *satī* was discussed widely in European publications as a "Hindu custom." And in 1829, with the help of Hindu reformers, the British prohibited it by law in their territories. In independent India, it is a crime. However, a shocking incident of a young woman's *satī* occurred in Rajasthan in 1987. This led to much stricter laws with no further reported occurrence. While *satī* was abolished almost two centuries ago, the life of an upper-caste widow remained difficult until recently. She was not remarried. She had to wear a white or dark color attire and was not allowed to put on heavy jewelry. She had to practically turn into a nun living within a household. I sadly recall the tears of a relative whose mother was widowed in her early 20s and had to be clad in simple clothes even at weddings and festivals. The woman was financially independent. But she could not even think about remarriage. The situation has changed now. Young (even older) upper-caste widows often get remarried, many encouraged by their in-laws who also offer support in raising children. State and central governments also have set up pension plans for them. However, poor elderly widows without relatives are still seen in a few pilgrimage towns living in beggars-like conditions. A few women's organizations like Maitri (https://www.maitriindia.org/) have now taken up their cause.

With the centrality of family life in the Hindu tradition, a Hindu woman's position as a wife and a mother is given most attention in various discourses. Yet there is one avenue outside of family life that extraordinary women have followed receiving immense respect within the society. This is the path of complete dedication to spiritual quest through devotion (*bhakti*), meditative practices as a renouncer, or social service. In an early Upanishad, a woman sage named Gargi is recognized as an equal in knowledge about Brahman to the most learned men of the time. In considering vernacular texts, we saw that many regional medieval saint-poets who spread the message of devotion were women. Their enduring popularity and stature for centuries indicate that spiritually advanced women's words are regarded highly by Hindus in all strata of the society. In more recent times, several female gurus have also been recognized for their spiritual achievements and have large following (literally thousands for some) in India and internationally. They are distinctive on the global scene in their influence as women. These female gurus work outside of widely followed Hindu social norms. But they are firmly rooted in the Hindu tradition. They draw on the traditionally set spiritual goals for ascetics, and as Karen Pechilis points out, "deemphasize their sexuality." Two Hindu concepts contribute to their rise as spiritual mentors: (a) *śakti* and (b) inner purity attained by following ascetic discipline. Centers of several women gurus also run social service (*sevā*) projects such as free kitchens, schools, etc. in different parts of the world, endowing them with the status of a beloved motherly figure. We will meet one such guru in a later chapter. A strikingly innovative path that women have begun to tread in India and in other countries is that of priesthood, considered a bastion of Brahmin men for two millennia. In the city of Pune in Maharashtra, two institutions – Shankar Seva Samiti and Jnana Prabodhini – have been established for the training of female priests who are just as proficient in their profession as their male counterparts and are enthusiastically invited by people. In Europe and America too, several women are now temple priests and perform rites of passage ceremonies, inverting the earlier restrictions. In fact, women priests see themselves as reclaiming their Vedic heritage. In 2018, I had an opportunity to hear the recitation of Vedic mantras by a woman who is in high demand in Maharashtra and found it extremely impressive.

As the above brief overview and some parts of the previous chapter show, women's roles in the Hindu society have been variegated and often paradoxical. In some ways, Hindu women's lives have been kept under the control of male relatives, especially husbands. At the same time, they have worked shoulder to shoulder with men of their families, been first transmitters of religion to their children, and some have even emerged as icons of spirituality, guiding thousands. As I have discussed elsewhere, in the twenty-first century, one challenge for Hindu women is to resist the manipulative use of selected passages in sacred texts to subordinate them, a trend that has long prevailed. But the other equally important challenge is to claim and employ in their lives those aspects of their religion that enable them to live to their full potential (as women priests are doing), while also drawing from secular feminist discourses.

GOALS FOR LIFE – MEN AND WOMEN

To a certain extent, the religious goals of Hindu individuals have been tied to their gender and caste roles because performing one's duties in the society is considered foundational for a good life. Some regulations for each category of people are also included in *dharma* texts like Manu. While a great deal of social privilege is given to Brahmins, there are also more extensive regulations for them. A Brahmin, for example, is required to avoid certain foods, and prohibited to ridicule poor, uneducated, or disabled people (at least as per texts). Beyond such caste-specific behavior, however, a range of moral and spiritual avenues, which are rooted in a few important metaphysical concepts, are open to all. Two broadly related concepts that frame moral values and life's goals are *saṃsāra* and *karma*. Within the expansive cycles of cosmic time that we considered earlier, created beings also go through cycles of life. They are born numerous times in different forms – human or animal. This is – *saṃsāra* – cyclical nature of life and death. Within these cycles, each deed (*karma*) leads to its inevitable consequence. One's present condition is a result of previous actions based on moral choices in the current or an earlier lifetime. In this schema, a powerful or high-status person with bad *karma* would be reborn in unfavorable conditions as human, animal, or insect. A person with low status with good *karma* would be reborn in favorable situations in the next birth. These ideas are woven in sacred narratives and heard recurrently in everyday expressions. They have paradoxical implications. On the one hand, a belief in the principle of *karma* gives solace to a person facing misfortune that their present moment can be a result of something they did in the past life; but by following a righteous path now, they would be in a better situation in the next life. On the other, it can also be used to explain away someone else's distressing circumstance such as caste discrimination to be a result of previous *karma*. In both types of usages, the stress remains on following the righteous path with appropriate goals in the present life. What are these appropriate goals?

In the Hindu view, whether articulated in elite Sanskrit or informal vernacular expressions, a well-lived life is marked by completion of four pursuits (*puruṣārthas*): *dharma* (duty/virtue/

moral self-fulfillment), *artha* (acquisition of worldly means/success), *kāma* (fulfillment of desires/sexual life/pleasure), and *mokṣa* (liberation/total freedom/end of rebirths). While the fourth of these is the ultimate spiritual goal, its direct pursuit by renouncing the world is not recommended for all. That path is only for exceptional individuals. An average person should fulfill the first three before pursuing *mokṣa*. Among the other three, *artha* − production of wealth and worldly success − is important for self-worth, supporting the family, and sustaining the society. But acquisition of wealth must be honest; this is the highest form of purity (Manu 5.106). *Kāma* is important for progeny and full development of life. Body as the basis of action, and mind as a means for cultivation of the self, should not be deprived of pleasure. Enjoyment of food, arts, loving relations, etc. enriches life. But pleasure should not be unrestrained; otherwise, it can lead to a chaotic life. The foundational (holding all together) pursuit of life, however, is *dharma*, generally understood as performing one's duty and following a moral path. It must be integrated in the pursuit of *artha* and *kāma* as well. A part of a person's duties includes honestly carrying out one's assigned work as per social position and fulfilling duties within family. We saw an example of this in the Introduction with Govind, Rukma's husband, who visits his parents every evening as his *dharma*. The other part is following norms of ethical behavior and moral values. As Wendy Doniger points out, the moral values prescribed in texts like Manu (2.87, 6.92, 10.63) for Brahmins can be seen as normative for others. These are also amply conveyed in Sanskrit and vernacular narratives, couplets, and songs functional in everyday life. Important values include truthfulness, kindness, generosity, humility, friendliness to all, keeping one's word, serving guests and elders, and making sacrifices for others. It is when one has fully completed one's duty within the society and achieved the three goals of *dharma*, *artha*, and *kāma*, one is ready for liberation or *mokṣa*, which requires complete detachment from worldly matters and reaching an elevated spiritual state by dedicated following of meditational/contemplative or other religious practices.

In *dharma* treatises, various phases of life are presented as appropriate for pursuing the above goals. In these texts, a lifetime is divided into four stages of being (a) a celibate student (*brahmacarya*),

(b) a householder (*gṛhastha*), (c) a retiree living in the forest (*vānaprastha*), and (d) renouncing the world (*sanyāsa*). Each stage, called *āśram*, has a specific emphasis. In the first, gaining knowledge appropriate for a hereditary profession is the focus. In ancient India, a male child (Brahmin and Kshatriya) left home to study with a teacher at around eight or learned skills from family members; female children learned skills from mothers. The norm for a pupil is to learn and behave respectfully with the teacher. In the householder stage, which is considered the most important because it supports the society, the norm is to pursue *artha* and *kāma* while being true to one's *dharma*. In this phase, a person would get married, raise a family, and acquire wealth to contribute to the society. Householders would also fulfill obligations to parents and ancestors, perform appropriate ceremonies, and may seek a spiritual guide. Around the age of 50, a person is expected to begin to withdraw from the worldly life, transfer wealth and obligations to children (sons), and live a retired life. This is a kind of transitional phase to the last phase beginning around 72 when a person is expected to become completely detached and focus on the ultimate spiritual goal of liberation. Combined with the system of *varṇa*, this schema of *āśrams* has come to be known as *varṇāśram dharma*. It is unlikely that many followed it verbatim in any era, but it has long provided a general framework for organizing society and life. For Hindus of any caste, one's duty to family and society during active years and gradually withdrawing from worldly affairs to focus on spiritual advancement with age serve as important guidelines for life.

The above survey of Hindu social organization, women's roles, and life goals indicates that they are layered and often paradoxical. So, how does a Hindu person navigate their moral/ethical choices within this ethos? Keeping in view two aspects of the tradition helps us understand this. First, while the injunctions in *dharma* treatises have been influential and contributed greatly to severe caste discrimination for two millennia, neither these nor any other sacred texts contain commandments. Nor are Brahmins, the traditional custodians of these texts, have been in charge of regulating people's personal or community lives. A text like Manu has not been a functional religious text like narratives of epics and Puranas or songs of saint-poets in vernaculars. Most Hindus do not even know of Manu's text let alone read it. As a genre, the *dharma* texts are so embedded in the political/material culture of antiquity that people would not be able to relate to them even if they tried. Narratives and songs are much more relatable. Therefore, taking texts like Manu as fixed "law" leads us away from the ground realities of their usage in everyday life of Hindus. While activists resisting caste oppression and demanding more rights for women rightly object to some passages in Manu's text, overall, as Olivelle aptly observes, there is more "heat" than "light" in debates surrounding it. Second, which arises from the first, is that in the absence of commandments or an authority figure, people make moral decisions based on their knowledge of religious sources like sacred narratives, customs of their communities, guidance from a guru figure, and their own conscience. Since the concept of heresy or blasphemy is not operative in Hinduism, it is generally possible to uphold one's moral choice if it does not transgress too far from the customs of one's caste.

We will end this chapter by looking at the process of making moral choices by a low-caste woman, Jashoda (not real name), whom I knew closely for many years. Jashoda was a young woman whose mother worked in the water-hut (room with drinking water) of an educational institution in a small town in India. Belonging to a caste very low in the hierarchy and with little money, she had no education and was married off soon after her father died. The husband drove her out of home when he fell for another woman. Jashoda came back to her mother. But she too died soon, leaving Jashoda with the responsibility of two younger brothers. Jashoda took her mother's job to fulfill her *dharma* to her two adolescent brothers. But in dealing with them and the ex-husband who had begun to harass her, she had to make some tough decisions (such as remarrying outside of her caste) that would not be easily approved by her elders. Jashoda was known as an upright woman and a devotee of a local goddess whom her community worshipped. She performed *pūja* (worship ceremony) for the goddess daily. When she had to make an important decision, she would consult women whom she trusted and think about the matter during prayers. She would then come to a firm decision. She would present her decisions to her brother and community elders as inspired by the goddess (a euphemism for her conscience). After some back and forth, she was always able to convince them of the propriety of her choices. Jashoda lived with the dignity of a working woman, married a person of her choice, supported her brothers for long even after her remarriage, and volunteered her time in free cataract camps as social service. One could hear her singing her favorite vernacular devotional songs all the time. She of course did not know the Sanskrit terms for all the *puruṣārthas* except *dharma* in colloquial Gujarati – *dharam*. She referenced her choices using that term – highlighting its foundational significance in Hindu life. By the time I last saw her, Jashoda had successfully completed the goals of *artha*, *kāma*, and *dharma*. She is still not old enough to think about the fourth goal of *mokṣa*.

Table 4.1 Important terms related to Hindu social organization and life goals

	Related Sanskrit terms	Meaning
Caste	varṇa	lit. color, broad category of classification – Brahmin, Kshatriya, Vaishya, and Shudra
	jāti	Regionally based occupational community
	Dalit	"Trampled upon," communities considered "untouchable," outside of the caste system and lowest in the social hierarchy
	panchāyat	Council of leaders (of a caste)
Women	pativratā	A woman dedicated to husband
	satī	Woman who climbs husband's funeral pyre, also the act
	śakti	Energy (cosmic)
Moral pursuits and life goals	Samsara	The phenomenal world in which cycles of birth and death occur
	karma	Deed, action (generally based on moral choice)
	puruṣārtha	Appropriate pursuit
	dharma	Moral duty
	artha	Financial/worldly success
	kāma	Desire, pleasure
	mokṣa	Liberation (from rebirth)
Stages of life	āśram	Stage of life
	brahmacarya	Celibate studentship
	gṛhastha	Householder
	vānaprastha	Retired (in a forest)
	sanyāsa	Renouncing

FURTHER EXPLORATION SUGGESTIONS

Daniélou Alain. 1993. *Virtue, Success, Pleasure & Liberation: The Four Aims of Life in the Tradition of Ancient India*. Rochester, VT: Inner Traditions International.

NDTV (India). 2008. "Pune Embraces Female Hindu Priests." Video. 1:41. Accessed July 13, 2022. https://www.youtube.com/watch?v=nQm EMnD3dfY.

Olivelle, Patrick. 1998. "Caste and Purity, A Study in the Language of Dharma Literature" *Contributions to Indian Sociology*, 32: 189–216.

Pechilis, Karen. 2004. *The Graceful Guru: Hindu Female Gurus in India and the United States*. New York, NY: Oxford University Press.

Pintchman, Tracy, and Rita DasGupta Sherma, eds. 2011. *Woman and Goddess in Hinduism: Reinterpretations and Re-Envisionings*. New York, NY: Palgrave Macmillan.

Smith, Brian K. "Varṇa and Jāti." In *Encyclopedia of Religion*, 2nd ed., edited by Lindsay Jones, 9522–9524. Vol. 14. Detroit, MI: Macmillan Reference USA, 2005. *Gale in Context: U.S. History*. Accessed July 8, 2022. https://link.gale.com/apps/doc/CX3424503250/UHIC?u=mlin_m_wellcol&sid=bookmark-UHIC&xid=691475c8.

Sugirtharajah, Sharada. 1998. "Women in Hinduism." In *Themes and Issues in Hinduism*, edited by Paul Reid-Bowen, 56–79. London: Cassell.

Teltumbde, Anand. 2020. *Dalits: Past, Present and Future*, 2nd ed. Abingdon, Oxon: Routledge.

Vedanta New York. 2017. "What Is My Duty in Life? | Swami Sarvapriyananda" Accessed July 9, 2022. Video. 7:21. https://www.youtube.com/watch?v=ktPaG5hydQk.

5

RELIGIOUS ACTION AND EXPRESSIONS

In the absence of a singular scripture, set of commandments, or binding belief, at the core of Hindu life is religious action. For a Hindu, what she/he does, or expresses, is more important in the religious context than any authoritative belief system. Rituals, art, performances, ethical action, and mediation form a major cluster of channels through which significant Hindu values and concepts are expressed and sustained. As in other areas of Hinduism, religious actions and expressions (including religious art) are also intricately layered and diverse. One may witness grand worship rituals in large temples with royal patronage in the morning, and the same evening the lighting of a lamp under a tree by a Dalit or tribal woman as a form of prayer. At lunchtime, one may see people serving food to hundreds in a community kitchen (*annakshetra*) or a housewife feeding a cow, a dog, or birds in front of her house as a religious act. Within this striking diversity, however, a thread running through most is an aspiration to make auspicious what is here and now, to invite sacred powers to bless this moment of life or to purify the mind. Only some actions are undertaken with the explicit aim of liberation from the phenomenal world. In this chapter, we will look at some widely prevalent genres of religious action that are loosely associated with the three paths – *jnāna*, *bhakti*, and *karma* –

DOI: 10.4324/9781315303352-6

considered valid for spiritual growth by Hindus. We will also consider expressions of religious ideas and emotions through art. As we have been doing, we will consider both the elite practices overseen by figures with authority and informal popular practices with greater agency of lay performer/s. In each section, we will begin with Sanskrit-based elite practices found widely all over India and elsewhere. We will then consider examples of informal religious activities of lay people, which have immense diversity based on regional and community customs.

RELATING TO THE DIVINE PALPABLY

IMAGES AND DIVINE PRESENCE

As we have seen, the Hindu sacred world is occupied by a host of divinities, some worshipped across the Hindu world, and some are regional/local. Sects devoted exclusively to a single deity such as Shiva, Krishna, Vishnu, the goddess, etc. or even a saintly figure are followed by a percentage of Hindus. But a large percentage of them are non-sectarian. They worship various deities as representing different aspects of the divine or the Ultimate in different contexts. In this broad survey, we will not look at sect-specific practices; but only consider the basics of Hindu worship.

At the heart of several Hindu worship practices are images, earlier called "idols." Because of the derogatory connotations associated with "idolatry," however, now scholars use the term "image." As Diana Eck has insightfully shown, Hinduism is an "imaginative" and "image-making" religious tradition. Hindus believe that with immeasurable grace, the divine makes himself/herself accessible to worshippers in images, places, and even in the form of holy people. The indigenous term for "image" is *murti*, related to the Sanskrit term *murta* meaning "manifest" or "incarnate." The Tamil Sri Vaishnava tradition uses the term *archāvatār*, meaning "divine descent for worship." A wide variety of images of the divine are worshipped by Hindus. Some are anthropomorphic (human-like) with added features indicating their superhuman status. Many images of Shiva, Vishnu, the Goddess, and other deities, for example, have multiple arms; Hanuman has the head of a monkey and

Ganesha the head of an elephant. These kinds of images follow iconographic conventions embedded in the narratives contained in the epics and the Puranas. The other types of images are aniconic or symbolic. Some of these – such as Shiva's image as a shaft, a geometric design for the goddess, etc. – also follow iconographic prescriptions of sacred texts. An image of a deity can be made in stone, wood, metal, or other materials. Small images of both anthropomorphic and symbolic types may also be installed in a home shrine. Govind Kulkarni, Rukma's husband whom we met in the Introduction, worships such images. In addition to man-made images, a grove, a rock outcropping or a tree, may be recognized as having sacred presence and worshipped by local people; and may become more widely popular over time. Some images are ritually consecrated, and some are not. But the divine is believed to be manifest in every sacred image when invited with *bhakti* and can be engaged using all senses including *mana* (mind). With this belief, an image of a deity is treated like a divine guest in the given context and is offered hospitality appropriate for her/his heavenly stature. This form of worship is called *pūjā*.

PŪJĀ IN TEMPLES

Hindu temples are seen as residences of deities where their images – anthropomorphic or aniconic – are installed after a ritual of consecration. Depending on patronage, temples vary in their sizes and the *pūjā* routines. There are also a few distinct components of *pūjā* for each deity. But here we will consider only the basic features of temple *pūjā*. In the temple context, the image of the deity is first consecrated and then installed in a chamber called *garbhagṛha* located deep in the temple. This is the abode of the deity. The *pūjā* performed in a grand or midsize temple is formal in nature. It is performed by one or more appointed priests (generally Brahmin men) and has several components in its daily routine, beginning at dawn and generally ending with the ceremony when the deity retires for the day. In several temples, these include waking the deity up, giving them a bath, presenting a beautiful attire, flowers, and jewelry as *śṛṇgār* (dressing up), offering food or *prasād* (which can be simple or elaborate), expressing reverence in various ways, and closing the *garbhagṛha* at night when the deity goes to sleep (Figure 5.1).

For each component there are Sanskrit mantras chanted by the priest who is called *pūjāri*. The most public ritual of honoring the image is *āratī*, waving of lamps around the image. During this

Figure 5.1 Pūjā in a temple in Pune, Maharashtra.
Photograph by author.

ritual, a Yak-tail fan is also waved to keep the deity cool. Large crowds of people attend it. In *āratī*, after a few Sanskrit mantras, generally a hymn in the regional language is also sung in chorus by all attending devotees to the accompaniment of drums, bells, or other instruments. The singers also keep the beat with claps. The ritual is seen as incorporating the five foundational elements of the cosmos – the earth (with flowers), water (moved around the lamps at the end), fire (with the flame), air (with Yak tail-fan), and space (with incense). On completion of the ceremony, the priest or a participant brings the lamp/s to the attendees who circle their hands over the flame and touch their eyes with them. The flowers and food offered to the deity are distributed among the participants as representing divine blessings.

If *pūjā* rituals in temples are performed by priests, the ostensible question is: What does an average Hindu do in a temple? Well, Hindus go to a temple to visit its divine resident. They take off their shoes outside the temple. Every temple has a bell at the entrance that the visitor rings as she/he enters, as a signal to the mind that she/he is entering a sacred place. Then the worshiper walks deeper into the temple toward the *garbhagṛha*. She/he stops outside of the *garbhagṛha* with folded hands and has the *darśan* (viewing) of the deity, which is the main purpose of the visit. This is a special kind of viewing – not just looking at the glory of the deity in all finery, but exchange of glances with the divine manifest in the image. The eyes of anthropomorphic images are prominent; and even the aniconic images like the shaft (*liṅga*) representing Shiva have eyes drawn on them with sandalwood paste or some such material. It is believed that as the visitor looks at the image, especially the eyes, the divine reciprocates the glance as a form of blessing. After that the worshiper may close her/his eyes in prayer and bow (Figure 5.2).

But the reciprocal viewing is at the center of the visit. After *darśan*, if it is an appropriate time, the visitor partakes of the *prasād*. Before leaving, she/he may or may not offer money in the gift box and may or may not speak briefly with the priest whose role is not to preach or lead a prayer but mainly to perform *pūjā*. For a Hindu, visiting a temple is a personal experience of connecting with the divine, regulated only by the temple hours. A person may visit a

Figure 5.2 Woman bowing to images of Rama, Sita, Laxman, and Hanuman in a temple.

Photograph by author.

temple daily, at regular intervals or only occasionally. Many daily visitors prefer the *āratī* time for the opportunity to participate in singing. A temple may organize lectures by spiritual teachers that worshippers may attend. There is no membership or mandatory contribution in a temple, nor is participation in rituals by visitors required. Followers of other religions who are used to organized prayer services often find a Hindu temple chaotic with people entering and leaving constantly. But a Hindu prizes the deeply personal nature of her/his visit.

A note about caste is necessary here. Until recently, a large number of temples prohibited entry to Dalits. With caste discrimination being punishable by law in independent India and people moving to different parts of the country, such is not the case at most temples now. However, there are still reports of a Dalit person being asked or forced to leave temple premises at times. This is more common in some areas of India than others. Legally, such cases can be reported to the local police, but it remains uncertain how many are. On the other hand, perhaps as a way of atonement, a few major temples are inviting members of Dalit and other lower-caste communities to join their management teams. A close Dalit acquaintance of mine has been a managing trustee of a prominent temple for years and has played a key role in putting progressive policies in place there.

PŪJĀ AT ROADSIDE SHRINES

In any city, town, or village of India and Nepal, one is bound to see multiple small shrines on the roadside. Some of these may be small structures built in stone or brick; some may be completely open with a sacred object recognizable only with presence of *pūjā* materials in front. Unlike bigger temples built by kings or wealthy patrons, roadside shrines are built phase by phase entirely by worshippers who install an image or discover an aniconic sacred object at the spot. Once a devotee begins to pray and offer simple *pūjā* – just lighting a lamp, offering flowers, and putting a small amount of sugar or coconut in the front of the image – people begin to notice, bow their heads, and make offerings there. There is no appointed Brahmin priest; and worshippers are generally from the lower socioeconomic strata. The deity is usually a village god/goddess identified as a local manifestation of Shiva, Krishna, the great goddess etc. who are worshiped widely in the Hindu world. Often a narrative about the deity appearing in the dream of a devotee is heard. People may take turns, or a community member may take the responsibility of performing the daily *pūjā*, which is simple with chanting in the regional language. People do what they know and can afford. Some roadside shrines grow bigger over time and may even turn into small size temples. *Pūjā* at roadside shrines can be seen as one of the most democratic expressions of Hindu faith in public areas.

Manju whom we met in Introduction worships at such a shrine. Jashoda whom we met in the last chapter has been a major contributor to such a roadside shrine-turned-temple. When I knew Jashoda years ago, she would stop every day at a roadside shrine of the local goddess Meladi on her way to work. She would bow, offer carefully picked flowers, and offer a coin or two on some days. On festival days, she would even offer a small scarf or sweets. She had immense faith in mother Meladi and sought inspiration from the goddess in making all major decisions in life. When I last visited her town in 2006, the roadside shrine where she prayed was a small but nicely built temple and the person performing *āratī* was none other than Jashoda's husband who is neither from her caste nor from the region. Even with hierarchies of caste, the freedom to establish a deeply personal relationship with a preferred deity without the intervention of a priest offers religious agency to Hindus like Jashoda and her husband, which they highly value.

Roadside shrines to local deities abound in all regions of India. Goddess Mansa in Bengal, male deity Khandoba in parts of Maharashtra and Karanataka, goddess Mariamman in Tamil Nadu, the protective Golu Devta of Uttarakhand, goddess Khodiyar of Gujarat, Ramdev Peer in Rajasthan and scores of other regional divinities form the centers of religious lives of local communities. In February 2019, Sri Lanka's *Sunday Observer* carried a story about roadside Ganesha shrines set up by poor Hindu tea estate workers in this majority Buddhist country. People feel a special bond with them because their myths/legends generally have a close link to the region, and the deities are believed to effectively answer prayers with regard to various problems in worshippers' lives. Some of these deities may have been local heroes or revered women who later became deified. Initially worshipped as a partial manifestation a pan-Hindu god/goddess, a regional deity may gain an independent status over time and their worship may spread much wider. In my research on goddess Khodiyar, a ninth-century deified woman from Saurashtra in Gujarat, I found that as her devotees settled in England and America, she also found a place in London and New York Hindu temples. In some cases, the religious affiliations of the deity may be fluid. For example, Ramdev Pir of Rajasthan, remembered as a prince who was especially kind to the downtrodden, is deeply venerated by Hindus and Muslims of the region. Similarly, Jhulelal, worshipped by Sindhi Hindus, is also revered as Khwaza Khizr by Muslims.

These regionally worshipped figures throw light on some important basics of Hinduism. First, the process of integration of local deities into the broader circuits of worship offers a pointer to understanding how the process of expansion of the Hindu pantheon since the Puranic period has occurred. Secondly, the shrines of deified heroes and women worshipped by Hindus and non-Hindus alike offer a glimpse into what religion encompasses at grassroots level. It is linked to people's immediate needs of everyday life rather than to ideological debates about religious identity that get political coloring. Some scholars like Sree Padma have drawn attention to worship of local deities. However, the evolving nature of *pūjā* at roadside shrines demands more extensive study as a core component of Hinduism since it forms a major religious practice of large masses of Hindus (Figure 5.3).

Figure 5.3 Left: Roadside shrine turned temple of a local goddess in Western India. Right: Home shrine, Kumaon, Uttarakhand.

Photographs by author.

PŪJĀ AT HOME

Most practicing Hindus – rich and poor, upper-caste and lower-caste, men and women – also perform *pūjā* at home. A household may have a small metal or wood shrine with small images; or it may be just a counter with glossy printed pictures of deities. These images are generally not consecrated with a formal ritual. But the area becomes sacred for the family. Everyday a member of the family performs *pūjā*. In Rukma's family, her husband Govind has taken that responsibility. *Pūjā* at home may be performed with Sanskrit chants, with vernacular hymns or none at all. They also do not follow complex ceremony routines. It is generally offered only once during the day with some shared components with temple *pūjā* such as offering flowers and food and lighting a lamp. On special occasions like birthdays or festivals, home *pūjā* is more elaborate. In addition to *pūjā*s performed in the above manner, practices such as *rangoli* (performed by women like Rukma in the morning), lighting a lamp by the waterpot in the house or basil plant in front of it are also seen as forms of worship. In home *pūjā*, its regularity is given most importance because it is believed that it fills the home with divine blessings.

CROSSING OVER TO THE SACRED

The locations for *pūjā* discussed above are generally parts of people's regular routines – familiar and easily reachable. But for centuries, specific locations are perceived to have immense sacred power, and generally reached with effort. Such a place is called a *tīrtha* (lit. river ford), derived from Sanskrit verb *tṛ* (to cross over). One crosses over from the mundane phenomenal world to the realm of the sacred. In Vedic literature, the word did not have a sense of a place of pilgrimage but did have an association with purity and rituals that help humans to connect with sacred powers. Ritual purity was thought of as akin to river waters, which flowed from heavens to the earth and bridged the two. The term *tirtha* points out the significance of rivers and water bodies in general as purifying places since ancient times. Some rivers like the Ganga, the Yamuna, the Narmada, and the Godavari have special status as sacred bodies of water. A large number of *tīrtha*s that have developed in association with divine beings in the *Ramayana*, the *Mahabharata*, and the Puranas since the classical Hinduism period are also on riverbanks. Some are on mountaintops, in caves, in forests, and at seashores, all of which have association with inner purity in Hindu imagination. Only some *tīrtha*s have now become parts of busy city neighborhoods. The close association of nature with sanctity in Hinduism is often referenced by religious leaders and environment activists in their calls for climate protection.

Major Hindu *tīrtha*s related to the narratives also create sacred circuits that link at different locales in South Asia. Those associated with the *Ramayana*, for example, link in city of Ayodhya on the banks of river Sarayu in north India (Rama's capital), the hills of Chitrakoot (where he lived in exile), Pampa lake where he met Hanuman, and Rameshwar in south India that faces Lanka. Similarly, there are 12 sites in different parts of India where Shiva is believed to have manifested as a shaft of light, as per Puranas. According to another narrative in the Puranas, when Shiva's wife Sati immolated herself in anger because her father did not invite her husband, he (Shiva) moved around with his wife's body neglecting his duty. Vishnu had to finally cut parts of Sati's body to bring Shiva back to his divine self. The 51 sites where Sati's body parts are believed to have fallen became sacred seats of *śakti*. The Puranas contain extensive passages extolling the virtues of these *tirtha*s as bestowers of spiritual merit. These texts are known as *mahātmya* (glorification). With integration of regional deities into the Hindu pantheon, their composition is still ongoing, often in vernaculars. The place/s of worship of local gods may acquire an important *tīrtha* status over time. The new circuits create miniature sacred landscapes, again generally close to nature where one can perform rites for worldly or spiritual benefits.

One of the most important benefits of performing sacred rites at *tīrtha*s, as per *mahātmya*s, is related to death and the deceased.. Dying at some *tīrtha*s is said to automatically free one from cycles of rebirth. Banaras/Kashi on the banks of river Ganga, considered an abode of Shiva, is one of the most sacred places of this type where many Hindus arrive before death. A dip in the river is believed to wash off bad *karma*s and open the door for *mokṣa*. For performing rites for the peace of deceased ancestors, Gaya in Bihar is seen as an ideal site. Many people living far away from these places, however, are not able to visit such places. For them, local circuits serve the purpose. Each region has sites that are believed by locals to have sanctity similar to the haloed *tīrtha*s. Besides the aim of getting spiritual benefits, another major reason for pilgrimage is thanksgiving. Newlyweds make a pilgrimage to their *kuldevī*'s (family goddess) *tīrtha*; people make pilgrimages to thank deities for success in studies or profession. In recent times, with development of transportation facilities and economic growth, pilgrimage centers are thriving. Many pilgrimage places have also developed aspects of tourism to attract young visitors. Several have their websites and offer online video *darśan* every day.

Hindu pilgrims have traveled through *tirthas* and traversed through various circuits for centuries, on foot, in bullock carts, and now in trains, buses, and even helicopters. Diana Eck suggests that their journeys have created links among pilgrimage sites in different corners of India and inscribed its physical landscape with sacred meanings. They come from all castes and classes. Like roadside shrines, places of pilgrimage, especially rivers and mountaintops, are open to all. Even at temples at such sites, the kind of discrimination experienced at times by Dalits locally (where people know one another's social background) is not prominently visible since racially, people of different castes are hardly distinguishable. We saw in the Introduction that Manju felt comfortable with the Kulkarnis while taking a dip in the Ganga in Haridwar. I have often met Dalits and even non-Hindus in the temple of Somnath (an important Shiva site) in Gujarat. What Eck has described as "locative piety" in Hinduism is indeed one of its most dynamic aspects as a religious tradition.

Yet with all its vibrancy, attachment to sacred locales has its complexities too. As mentioned in the chapter on the long history of Hinduism, India is home to diverse religious communities. As a secular democratic nation, it has a responsibility to all of them. As found at contested sacred sites worldwide, here too, claims of sanctity of some places by one community are countered by another for various reasons. Identity battles fought over sacred sites lead to sharp debates and sometimes violent encounters with devastating results for many people who have done no wrong. Hinduism has the dynamism of locative piety; but it also has profound teachings about detachment from the impermanent world in view of the vast cycles of creation and dissolution through which even divine beings pass. Some public figures are recommending turning to them and maintaining a balance between veneration of tirthas and a disciplined restraint in not making exclusive claims.

In addition to places, a holy person who can help one cross over from the worldly to the spiritual perspective on life is also treated as a *tīrtha*. Since ancient times, Hindu ascetics (*sanyāsīs*), holy men (*sādhus*) and women (*sādhvīs*), and *yogis* and *yoginis*, have traversed through or made their abodes outside of various towns and cities. Hindu householders give gifts of food and other things of basic necessity to them. And if a person gets a reputation of being learned and has the ability to guide people spiritually, she/he gradually is recognized as a guru figure and gets treated like a *tīrtha*. People visit them for *darśan* and touch their feet in veneration. These moving *tīrthas* may themselves visit their followers' habitats. So do deities residing in some temples on special occasions.

DIVINE ON THE STREET FOR DEVOTEES

So far, we have considered many ways in which devotees make efforts to relate to the divine. But there is also another channel offered by some major temples. They have divine images that are taken out on the streets to allow people from all strata of the society to have *darśan*. These temples have images in processions on special days and attract thousands of devotees every year. On designated days, the images are first worshipped inside the temple and then brought out in a procession through the streets on chariot/s or on poles carried by devotees. People gather in large numbers on the street to meet the divine visitors and the mood is celebratory. There are two well-known processions of this type – *rath yātra* (chariot procession) of the Jagannath (Krishna) temple in Puri, Odisa, and the procession of Nataraja (Shiva) temple in Chidambaram, Tamil Nadu. The former is replicated by devotees in the Hare Krishna movement in various parts of the world.

SEEKING THE DIVINE WITHOUT IMAGES

BHAKTI OF MIND

While *pūjā* and *darśan* are widely prevalent forms of Hindu worship, for many individuals spiritual quest takes other forms related to *bhakti* and *jnana* that do not involve images. A widespread practice of such *bhakti* is *jāp* or repetition of a mantra with or without a rosary (generally 108 times). Chanting a mantra audibly is believed to purify the mind and anchor it in remembering the divine. But inaudibly done *jāp* is believed to create mental vibrations that help spiritual progress and deepen *bhakti*. Some people follow what is called *mānas* (mental) *pūjā* in which they meditate on the deity and imaginatively make offerings. Many Hindus have a spiritual mentor (guru) who guides them to deeper levels of *bhakti*. A guru may give her/his disciples a specific mantra for *jāp*. Followers of a guru often gather in what is called a *satsang* (good company) for sharing and discussing spiritual matters. In these contexts, discussions often combine *bhakti* and *jnāna*.

Another extremely popular form of worship that does not necessarily involve images is singing vernacular devotional songs (*bhajans*) praising a god/goddess or exploring path to the formless divine in one's heart. This practice is generally informal in nature even though it can be formal in some contexts, especially when sung in a temple. *Bhajans* can be heard being sung by people while completing their daily chores – women cleaning their houses early in the morning, farmers working the fields, or a carpenter sawing his timber. Some people sing *bhajans* as a spiritual discipline every day. *Bhajan* singers may also gather in the evening in the village square and sing till late in the night on specific days. They view their practice as one of the most powerful forms of worship because it is grounded only on devotional sentiments and human voice. Not requiring any material offering, it is portable and an equalizing practice between the rich and the poor. Most individuals and groups have their favorite saint-poets. *Bhajans* of some saint-poets may get incorporated into rituals of specific sects. And *bhajans* of some saint-poets like Kabir become so widely popular that religious communities develop around them. For such communities, the *bhajans* of the saint-poet are foundational religious texts and have a formal status. But the same songs may also be sung by other people informally. A *bhajan* belongs to whoever sings it. Their musical aspects are discussed below.

MULTIPLE FORMS OF YOGA — BHAKTI, MEDITATION, ETHICAL ACTION

For Hindus, the aim of disciplined spiritual practice is to be united with the divine (if one worships a deity) or being absorbed in the Ultimate (Brahman) through inner search and experiencing complete freedom. This would finally lead to exhaustion of karmas and release from cycles of birth. Each path that leads to attaining this goal is a type of *yoga* (lit. "union"). The three main types of yoga to which people commonly refer are — *bhakti-yoga*, *jñāna-yoga*, and *karma-yoga*. The practices of relating to the divine discussed above — *pūjā*, listening to the praise of the deity, singing devotional hymns, *jāp*, etc. form aspects of what is called *navadhā* (ninefold) *bhakti* encompassing *śravaṇa* (listening to hymns), *kīrtana* (singing hymns), *smaraṇa* (remembering), *sevā* (serving), *archanā* (praising), *dāsyam* (being a servant), *sakhyam* (loving like a friend), and *ātmanivedana* or *prapatti* (complete surrender) to the divinity. Disciplined following of any of them is believed to lead to a union with the chosen deity or the divine in the depth of one's heart. This spiritual path is termed *bhakti-yoga*.

Another path is that of *jñāna-yoga*, often termed simply yoga. In the international context, what is often referenced as "yoga" is traditionally known as *hatha-yoga*, the disciplined channeling of energy through physical postures. In the Hindu spiritual context, it is a stage in *jñāna-yoga*, associated with inner search with contemplation and meditation. There is a general scholarly agreement that practice of this yoga predates the Vedic culture, as evidenced by the seals of the Indus Valley civilization. References to it are seen in Vedic literature. But its most well-known systematic exposition is found in sage Patanjali's treatise *Yogasutra* (dated between 400 BCE and 400 CE), recognized widely as the foundational text on spiritual yoga. This form of yoga is practiced by integrating bodily discipline, ethical behavior, and various layers of mental activities to reach a state of calmness and, ultimately, complete freedom. It is believed that in the ultimate state, called *samādhi*, the practitioner is a detached "seer" and liberated even from the disturbances of her/his own mind. She/he experiences the self in its pure state. This path is followed by Hindus who are more inclined toward the search within oneself. It closely parallels Jain and Buddhist practices of meditation. The calming techniques, leading to reduction of stress and clarity of thought, are also widely practiced by non-Hindus without seeing it as a religious path. Yoga schools, therefore, are now found all around the world.

While *bhakti* and *jñāna* help the cultivation of heart and mind, the third path, *karma*, comprises activities that give spiritual discipline a concrete form in the social context. As we saw in the last chapter, some values such as truthfulness, kindness, generosity, and keeping one's promises are stressed in *dharma* treatises, epics, and devotional songs. These values form the foundation for the fulfillment of one's duties (*dharma*) to one's family and society. To this end, it is expected that a person engages in activities that serve others. Philosophically, since every being is ultimately identical with Brahman, in serving others one connects with one's own inner self. Two types of activities are related to fulfillment of this expectation. The first is termed *sevā* (service) without any expectation of reward. *Sevā* is woven into the daily life of individuals in a variety of ways. An important form of it is attending to the needs of the elders or taking care of a family member when sick. A person who takes on these responsibilities for a long time is held in high regard. Serving parents in their old age is an ideal of *sevā* that children generally try to pursue. Traditionally, for a married woman, serving her husband and his family is considered a primary form of *sevā*. Women following the ideal are respected highly. But the ideal has also been widely manipulated, often to the extent of exploitation.

Sevā takes a variety of forms outside of the family. One may volunteer to offer services in a religious place like a temple or an *āśram* (hermitage or institution) of a guru. Or one may offer *sevā* according to one's ability (*yathā śakti*) as a volunteer in a hospital, animal shelter, or any context where help is needed. For example, during hot summers in India, many poor women and men set up water stalls with clay pots on roads and offer pedestrians water.

Whereas some well-to-do physicians give free services to the needy for two to four weeks every year as *sevā*, some people offer *sevā* during disasters. During the 2001 massive earthquake in Gujarat, when I was in the region for research, a number of temples and Hindu organizations set up camps for the impacted people as what they termed *mānav sevā* (service to humanity).

The significance of *sevā* is articulated recurrently in religious texts and by leaders. An often-quoted Sanskrit *subhaśita* (pithy nice saying) *sevā dharma prarma gahano, yoginām api agamya* ("the path of service is very deep, inaccessible even to *yogis*") from *Hitopadesha* ("Beneficial teaching," ca tenth century) places it above meditation. A similar motto, *sevā paramo dharma* ("service is the highest *dharma*"), is adopted by many organizations and schools, including the National Defence Academy of India. A parallel motto found in the *Mahabharata* and popularized by Gandhi in the twentieth century is *ahiṃsā paramo dharma* ("non-violence is the highest dharma") where the scope of non-violence includes *sevā*. Messages about service are also found in vernacular couplets cited by people in everyday conversations. Hindu leaders and gurus stress it in their teachings. The Hindu monk whose teachings inspired the establishment of early centers of Hindu philosophy in the USA, Swami Vivekananda, stressed the value of service by terming the disadvantaged *daridra nārāyaṇ* (the divine in the form of the needy). Most modern gurus have service projects conducted by their organizations. Many temples also have service projects, especially in the areas of education and health.

The second pillar of ethical action is *dāna* or "giving." Like everything in the Hindu ethos, *dāna* too takes a variety of forms some of which are informal and integrated into daily routines and some are formal and grand, getting a great deal of public attention. An important form of *dāna* since the Vedic era is *anna-dāna* (giving of food) to humans or animals. RV 10.17, for example, says "Bounteous is he who gives unto the beggar who comes to him in want of food, and the feeble." Perhaps embedded in difficulties of obtaining food for a stranded traveler in ancient times, the offering of food and hospitality to a visitor has become a widespread cultural value in the subcontinent among all communities. In the Hindu context, this type of *dāna* is performed regularly by women in many parts of India. If a holy man (of any religious affiliation), a beggar, or a Brahmin stops by the house asking for food, the woman of the house would try to give at least a small portion of food. In such a context, the giving of food is called *bhikśa*. Many observant women also place a portion of the food cooked for the day in a stone bowl outside of their homes for cows and other animals before they serve it to their family members. It is called *go-grās* (the morsel for the cow). Serving food to the family before this offering would be considered a breach of their accepted religious etiquette. Animals not only form parts of the divine pantheon's retinue, some street animals are treated with such care on a daily basis.

The formal practice of *anna-dāna* to large groups of people is observed at some big temples, pilgrimage sites, disaster relief camps, and often at commemorative events. In most of these contexts, food is given to anyone who arrives regardless of religious or caste affiliation. At the shrine of saint Jalaram in Virpur, Gujarat, on an average, 4,000 people are fed daily. Similarly, the Shanta Gajanan temple in Maharashtra, the Tirupati temple in Andhra, Jagannath temple in Puri, Orissa, Vaishnodevi temple in Jammu and scores of other temples distribute food (sanctified as an offering) to thousands of people. In the absence of structured membership, required tithe, and regulated visiting practice, the seeming inexhaustibility of food in Hindu temples is often found surprising by visitors. Hindus also collaborate with like-minded people and organizations in running similar projects in their own cities and in the diaspora. During the COVID-19 pandemic in 2020–2021, the UK communities following saint Jalaram joined hands with local businesses to offer food packages to the people in need. Similarly, in various cities in India, kitchens for stranded migrant laborers were opened. An organization inspired by Swami Prabhupad (founder of ISKCON) Akhaya Patra (https://www.akshayapatra.org/) addresses the issue of hunger and malnutrition among school children with their mid-day meal programs in partnership with state governments. In addition to food, the other types of giving include funds for education, hospitals, and clothing. *Sevā* and *dāna* are seen as the primary activities of a *karma-yogi*, the person who serves the divine by serving others. Such a person is recognized as pious whether or not she/he follows other religious activities like *pūjā* or meditation.

Karma-yoga does not involve following caste-specific behavior either. In modern times, several Hindus (a notable example being Gandhi) choose to follow this path, which has parallels with engaged Buddhism*, zakat* activities in Islam, charity in Christianity, and Catholic Liberation Theology.

SACRED MOMENTS IN A YEAR AND LIFE

FESTIVALS

As in religious traditions worldwide, in Hinduism too, people associate most dynamically with it during festivals, which allow joyful embodied experience of the sacred. Hindu festivals do not fall on the same date of the Gregorian calendar every year because they belong to lunisolar calendar systems. In different parts of India, two different lunisolar calendars are chiefly followed. One is "Vikram Samvat" (VS) and the other is "Shaka." These calendars have zero dates at 57 BCE and 78 CE, respectively, but they have the same names of months. Basically lunar, they get adjusted to the solar calendar every three years by adding a month. Festivals generally fall on specific days on the bright or dark lunar fortnight. But some festivals like the ones associated with the transition of the sun into Capricorn fall on Gregorian calendar dates. While various pan-Hindu festivals celebrated in different parts of the world are aligned to the lunisolar calendars, there are also some regional ones that align to local calendars such as Tamil sidereal and solar Bengal calendars.

Pan–Hindu festivals are linked to narratives about deities, sometimes more than one. The most well known of them, Diwali (festival of lights), celebrated for five days in the lunisolar months Aświn/Kārtik, has several narratives associated with it. As per the one associated with the Ramayana, Rama returned to his capital from exile on the new moon of Aświn. The elated subjects put lamps on his path, which became a "row of lights"– Diwali. Another narrative associates the festival with the goddess of prosperity, Lakshmi. It relates that when gods and non-gods were churning the milky ocean to get its jewels, the goddess emerged on this day. The festival is celebrated by Jains and Sikhs also with their own narratives. All three communities celebrate it with lighting of lamps, but associate different religious meanings to it. In Nepal it is celebrated as Tihar. With three communities celebrating the festival, the atmosphere comes dynamically alive in all parts of India. It also often leads to cordial exchanges among members of these communities at sweet, clothing, and jewelry shops, drawing attention to the significance of materiality in a religious ethos. In Nepal, Bali, and other parts of the world with sizable Hindu populations too, *pūjās* of Laxmi, Ganesha, Rama, and other deities are performed with much fanfare – with colorful *rangolīs* and exchange of sweets and fireworks.

While festivals like Diwali and Holi (festival of colors marking the beginning of the spring) are celebrated widely, they may not be the most important festival for a region. Important regional festivals align with changes in seasons and harvest cycles locally. They are linked to regional retellings of various myths. For example, Onam festival of Kerala is a regional harvest festival in which the narrative of Vishnu's measuring of three worlds in three steps and humbling king Bali appears with a modification. Bali appears here as a righteous local king who is punished for this arrogance but is allowed by Vishnu to visit his kingdom once every year on this day. In addition to diversity in narratives, the same festival is celebrated with different names and components in various parts of the Hindu world. The festival marking the end of the winter solstice is celebrated as Pongal in Tamil Nadu, Uttarayan in Gujarat, Makar Sankranti in several other regions, and Lohri in Punjab and mountainous north India. In different regions, it is celebrated with different festive components including foods. For Pongal, the main dish in Tamil Nadu is a sweet made of newly harvested rice and jaggery, in Gujarat it is a sesame and jaggery sweet, in Punjab it is jaggery bread. Jaggery made from sugar cane juice is common and mixed with regionally available ingredients. As is clear, differences of regional climate and cultures lead to great diversity in celebration of Hindu festivals. In fact, in many regional festivals, the region's culture (including food, performative and visual arts, clothing, etc.) and harvest cycles often provide the core elements to which pan-Hindu narratives get linked with modifications. Thus, even with variations in retellings, sacred narratives provide a thread that connects diverse regional Hindu festivals together.

Another thread that runs through festivities in diverse regions is the role of women in celebrations. With centrality of food, home decorations, clothing, and dance/music performances in festivities, women remain their chief facilitators. For a large number of people globally, the meanings of festivals are more closely linked to activities of women in their families than to religious meanings and worship practices. Such is the case in Hindu communities too. The Maharashtrian new year and spring festival, Gudi Padva (first day of the month of Chaitra), which is marked by hoisting of flag/scarf capped with a metal pot on a bamboo pole decorated with neem and mango leaves in front of the house, is Ravi and Chaitrali Kulkarni's favorite festival. While there are different narratives linked with it, for them its meaning is tied to the site of the Gudi as well as the aroma of stuffed sweet bread (*puran-poli*) and special lentil soup (Katachi Amti) both prepared by their mother. Rukma makes all the arrangements and cooks the festive food with Manju's help. The two women are happy working together, and Rukma sends a big share of the feast for Manju's family. Unspoken understandings of caste/class hierarchy and bonds of human relationships work simultaneously at festival times.

LIFE CYCLE RITUALS

The other set of sacred activities related to time are life cycle rites. In Hindu belief, life given by nature has to be molded by what is called *saṃskāra* – meaning "making perfect," "refining," "purifying," or "mental impressions." The term is closely related to *saṃskṛti*, which signifies "culture" or "civilization" – refinement of the society. Cultivation of good qualities in children by their parents or family is referred to as giving *saṃskāra*. A person also develops their own *saṃskāra* with their moral choices. These are the psychological aspects of *saṃskāra*. But the term *saṃskāra* also refers to life cycle rituals or rites of passage, which mark important moments or transitions in a person's life and make it meaningful. Ancient texts called *gṛhyasutra*s mentioned in Chapter 2 list different numbers of *saṃskāra*s – beginning with the parents decision to have a child.

Several of these *saṃskāra*s are performed at home; important ones are performed with attendance of relatives and friends. Not all of *saṃskāra*s have survived at verbatim since ancient times. But the following ones, starting before birth, are still widely performed and can be seen as basic.

The first is a ceremony before the birth of a child, called *sīmanta*. It is performed in the later stage of pregnancy for the would-be-mother with supplication for safe childbirth and also to cheer her up by showing support. A part of this ceremony is performed by the priest. But at its core is the pampering of the pregnant woman by female relatives. The first ceremony for the newborn, which is performed at home on the 11th or 10th day, is naming (*namkarana*). Traditionally, the name for the infant is chosen based on the birth sign according to the constellation of planets at the time of birth. In some communities, the name chosen by the parents is softly uttered by a female relative in the infant's ear. In the sixth or seventh month, the parents feed cooked food (generally rice) for the first time. In the ceremonies performed during the first year of life, some families involve priests, and some do not. An important ceremony for an upper-caste male child is sacred thread ceremony (*upanayana*), which in ancient times marked his departure from home to study with a teacher. This is an elaborate ceremony officiated by a priest. It continues to be performed as signifying initiation in education. However, some people choose not to perform it because of its discriminatory basis. The most important life cycle ceremony remains the wedding (*vivāha*), officiated by a priest. The mantras and many parts of the ceremony followed today are drawn from Vedic texts. A Hindu wedding is a commitment for life by the couple with Agni (fire) as the divine witness. Members of family – parents, siblings, and extended family members – also have assigned ritual roles. With origins in antiquity, the traditional ceremony has some ostensibly patriarchal parts. However, using the freedom for interpretation that takes into consideration the context, modifications are introduced by many priests (including women) for contemporary times. Some non-heteronormative weddings have also been performed with videos found on the internet. While they remain uncommon, people have begun to accept them gradually, focusing more on the commitment aspect of the ceremony. Once a couple has settled in the householder stage, their dream is to build a house. Often *vāstu* (architecture) experts are consulted to get guidance about auspicious directions of various parts of the house. The ceremony of entering a new house (*gṛhapraveś*) is performed to ensure good life in the house.

The last rite of a person, funeral with cremation, is called *antyeṣṭi*. With the belief in rebirth, death is seen as the soul leaving the earthly (*pārthiv*) body. After cremation, the ashes are flowed into sacred rivers. It is believed that with the funeral rites the earthly self merges into five cosmic elements. After death, rites called *śrāddha* are performed between the 9th and the 13th day for a peaceful transition of a deceased person's soul. These are repeated with a simpler version every year.

Many Hindu rites of passage are officiated by priests. But women play extremely important roles in all except the funeral. Their activities are not derived from Sanskrit texts. They are regional and community-specific celebratory parts with appropriate songs for each. It is interesting that in contemporary times, women have religious agency as gurus and even as priests; but in life cycle ceremonies, their roles are being cut short to make room for consumer market elements like DJ led dances and parties.

ART AND WORSHIP

As in all world religions, in Hinduism too, elite and popular art forms one of the most important channels for religious expression. It has long-established traditions of sacred architecture, sculpture, and performing arts. Two aspects related to religious art in the Hindu ethos draw our attention. First, art is considered inherently sacred. Rather than simply a channel for worship, it is a spiritual end in itself. The most celebrated theory of Indian aesthetics by the tenth-century Shaivite mystic Abhinavagupta likens the experience of aesthetic delight (called *rasa*) to the bliss experienced by a *yogī* in the highest spiritual state when a person experiences total freedom from all worldly entanglements. Second, among performing arts, along with music, dance was formally integrated into liturgy at major temples (especially with royal or aristocratic patrons) for long periods in history. Even though discontinued since the colonial ban on temple dancers, it continues to be performed within temple precincts at special events even today.

ARCHITECTURE

In the area of sacred architecture, the most important Hindu structure is a temple, called *devālaya* or *mandir* both connoting "divine abode." Dedicated to various deities, who are believed to reside in them (as images), temples have been centers of spiritual and social/cultural life of Hindu communities for centuries. Temples are found in all parts of the world where Hindus have lived or where Hinduism has had historical influence – India, Nepal, Bali, and several countries in South-east Asia. They did not exist during the earliest phase of Hinduism. In the early Vedic era, the main religious rituals were fire sacrifices performed in honor of Vedic deities at temporary brick altars. Scholars surmise that by the early century of the Common Era, influenced by grand Buddhist stone monuments that were patronized by royal courts, Hindu temples in materials such as timber likely came into existence. They perished with time. But remains of stone temples from around the fifth-century CE are extant. By the end of the first millennium, impressive temples, carved out of mountain sides or constructed from ground up, were found all around India. Prominent among these are rock carved temples in Mahabalipuram, Parthasarathy and Kapileshwar of Chennai, Khajuraho temples in central India, and the grand Yogyakarta temple in Java (Indonesia) where Hinduism had reached. By the mid-second millennium many more grand temples had been constructed with royal and aristocratic patronage. Temple building also continued during the Mughal era from the sixteenth through the early eighteenth century, often with patronage from royal courts. In contemporary times, grand temples are being built all over India and in various parts of the world with Hindu presence including Europe, Africa, America, and the middle east. Some of the most impressive among them are built by the Swaminarayan sect based in Gujarat.

Like altars of the Vedic era, a temple offers a link between the divine and the human worlds. It is a place where humans cross over to the spiritual world. For this reason, a temple is also seen as tīrtha.

Its significance as such is articulated architecturally with plans as specified in treatises called *vāstuśāstra*. The ground plan of a temple is called *Vāstupuruṣamaṇḍala*. It is a square geometric design divided into smaller squares and conceived as symbolizing the structure of the universe. The central square is the biggest and it is on this square that the *garbhagṛha* (sanctum sanctorum) is constructed. On the top of the *garbhagṛha* is a tower like superstructure that gets narrower as it rises, emulating a mountain. This is called *vimāna* in south India and *śikhara* (literally "the mountain top") in northern, western, and parts of eastern India. This is the tallest part of the temple. In front of the *garbhgṛha* are spaces or halls where worshippers stand for *darśan*, gather for communal singing of hymns, or sacred dance performances take place. A temple generally stands on an east-west axis. From the entrance, a worshiper walks deeper into the temple toward the deity in the *garbhagriha*, which is generally darker than the rest of the temple. It also has a path around it for circumambulation. The tower above the *garbhagṛha* is visible from a distance. The tower and the pathway leading to the *garbhagṛha* remind a visitor of a mountaintop and a cave, two places associated with meditation, representing inward movement and height of spiritual experience. The temple itself represents the cosmos arising out of the energy of the divine whose image is installed on the central square of the geometric ground plan.

Two styles of temple architecture in India are recognized as prominent: the southern style called *dravida* and northern style called *nagara* or *prasāda*. Both styles developed under the patronage of various royal dynasties. While both retain the fundamental principles of temple architecture, there are some notable differences. A north Indian temple may have more than one tower on various parts (halls) of the main building. The towers are curvilinear. There are generally no carved images on the towers, only simple designs. On the top of the tallest tower above the *garbhagṛha* is a disk with ridges on its rim. Above this is a *kalaś* (lit. water pot) with a pointed spire. This is the highest point of the temple right above the image and is believed to link the earthly and the divine realms. Some north Indian temples are large; but their premises are not as grand as those of prominent temples of south India. Major south Indian temples have well-defined boundaries of their premises that may be marked by tall gateway towers. Such a tower is called *gopuram*, which is generally taller than the tower of the main temple. A temple can have multiple *gopuram*s placed in a concentric pattern with the *garbhagṛha* as the center. A large temple premise can be like a section of a town with multiple passages and areas for various activities. The main building of a south Indian temple has only one tower. The *gopuram*s and towers of south Indian temples have a straight pyramid type of structure often with a barrel shaped top. They generally have multiple stories, each adorned with numerous images and mythical figures and can be very colorful. There are many subregional styles within these two broad categories. But there are also other distinctive regional styles. Many temples in the Himalayan regions and Nepal, for example, are in the pagoda style with tiered towers; temples in Kerala in the southwest have style with slanted rooftops; temples in Bengal mimic the local thatched roof residential style. With great diversity in the architectural styles, however, all Hindu temples remain abodes of deities where worshippers flock to meet them.

With regard to people who have agency in construction of temples, grand temples in the past relied on royal or aristocratic patronage and today rely on wealthy donors or fundraising activities. But the people who actually give shape to these grand monuments are architects and masons, often hereditary. Many communities in this category claim descent from the Vedic/Puranic deity Viśvakarma identified as the divine architect who created heavenly and some earthly cities. They minutely follow the manuals for temple architecture preserved for centuries. Yet as in the instances of numerous grand monuments over the world, only the patrons are well known.

SCULPTURE AND PAINTING

With the centrality of divine images in Hindu temples, sculpture is one of the most important religious arts in Hinduism. Art history scholar Vidya Dehejia points out that the earliest sculptures in the Hindu context may have been wooden or terracotta, which have not survived. But with the development of narrative literature from the last centuries before the Common Era, gradually the iconographic specifications for each deity in the Hindu pantheon emerged and began to be reflected in early images. Recently an Indian scholar has brought to light a small terracotta image of Ganesha belonging to the first-century CE with an elephant head, the most important aspect of the deity's iconography. Finely carved images of Vishnu, Shiva, Lakshmi, Durga, Ganesha, and other deities are found in some cave temples (carved on mountain sides) and constructed temples in Deogarh in north India, Elephanta and Ellora in Maharashtra, and Mahabalipuram in Tamil Nadu dating between the fifth and the eighth centuries. As in the area of temple architecture, precise prescriptions for carving images are contained in texts called *śilpaśātras*. A master sculptor, Ganapathi *sthapati* (sculptor/architect), explains in a video titled "Vaastu Marabu" (https://www.youtube.com/watch?v=AGn3HvGxR5g&t=116s) that for a *śilpi* (artist), the aim is to make the image graceful and come alive. While specific elements in the image of a deity such as the elephant head of Ganesha follow iconographic specifications, in the models for various parts of the human body standardization of proportion and shapes is found. Female arms, for example, resemble green bamboo and her torso an hourglass with a thin waist. For male figures, the torso is modeled after the front view of a bull's head. Eyes of images are generally large and have lotus petal or fish shape. The images of the deities installed for worship in temples are generally made of stone; but many temples also have images made of metal meant for processions on special days when the deities themselves go out to meet their devotees.

In addition to the image/s installed in the *garbhagrha*, the halls, ceilings, pillars, and outer walls of Hindu temples are covered with intricate carvings of floral, vegetation, and abstract designs, as well as animal and human figures in various contexts of real life – weddings, festivals, battles, royal processions, musical and dance performances, women putting on makeup, and even lovemaking. In south Indian temples, the towers are also completely covered with images. With the deity in the *garbhagrha* considered the source of life and the temple itself the universe, the surfaces are seen as its parts beaming with life. Some of the most exquisite sculptures are of women and celestial beings including divinities in dancing poses, which continue to inspire Indian classical dance styles even today.

Iconic and aniconic images are installed in Hindu neighborhoods during some festivals too. These are made by communities in the lower strata of the society who are paid or appreciated little compared to temple sculptors. Beautiful images of the goddess for Durgāpūjā, the most important festival for a majority of Bengali Hindus, for example, have been made for over 200 years by potters who live in narrow lanes in areas like the Kumartuli, Kolkata and often make the images in open streets. These are installed in numerous neighborhoods in all cities of Bengal and are worshipped for the nine nights with a great deal of enthusiasm. For the same festival celebrated as Navaratri in Gujarat, for centuries, potters of the region have been making clay pots with perforated surfaces. These are installed with lit lamps inside as images of the goddess in Hindu households. Images such as these are generally immersed in bodies of water at the end of the festival. Clay images of gods and goddesses are also made by various tribes living in forests. These include not only some pan-Indian deities but also several animals and heroes on horses. Here, the artists and worshippers are often the same people.

As far as painting is concerned, because of their perishable nature, especially in climate like that of South Asia, no evidence of ancient religious painting is found. Some scholars suggest however, that portable paintings called *charan-chitras* with sacred themes were likely in prevalence by the early centuries of the Common Era in all religious traditions of ancient India. Those are only inferred based on textual references. Early extant paintings in India are Buddhist paintings in the Ajanta caves in Maharashtra (seventh century). We do not find Hindu paintings until the beginning of the second millennium when the murals of Rajarajeshwar temple (1010 CE) were painted. Here, many painted figures mimic the sculpted images. One of the most productive periods in the area of painting came during the Mughal era and after its decline. Many artists trained in the workshops of Mughal courts dispersed to royal courts of Rajputana (to a great extent coterminous with present-day Rajasthan) and the Punjab and Himalayan mountain principalities. At the courts of these Hindu kings, they created exquisite miniature (small) paintings, a large number of which are based on Hindu narratives or religious poems. The paintings combine the clarity of lines, delicate human figures, and pastel colors as derived from Persian painting styles with some local motifs and stylistic features. Some of the most beautiful ones depict Krishna and Radha's love on the banks of the river Yamuna with the idyllic landscape of Braj adding a serene touch. For devotees, these paintings convey the spiritual dimension of love between the human heart and the divine. Some Rajput courts in the 16th and 17th centuries also developed distinctive painting styles. Originally found in royal manuscripts, today the paintings from this era are found in museums around the world and now also on the internet.

In the late nineteenth century, a major turn in Hindu religious painting came when affordable lithographs of paintings of Hindu gods and goddesses were introduced in the market. The most celebrated artist in this era was Raja Ravi Varma (1848–1906) who synthesized Hindu iconography with the European academic style and used Indian models to produce paintings that remain popular and in print (especially in calendars) till this day. Prominent among these is his depiction of goddess Lakshmi, which is found as an image in the *pūjā* area of many households. The inexpensiveness of these prints allows poor people to own them and has served as an equalizer to an extent. Another important equalizer has long been in the form of traditional folk/tribal paintings. Each region of India and Nepal has a folk painting style developed over centuries – Mithila (Bihar and Nepal), Kalighat (Bengal), Patachitra (Odisha), Gond (central India), Kalamkari (Andhra Pradesh), Phad (Rajasthan), etc. Most of these belong to people (women and men) in the lower strata of the society. The Mithila style (originally for wall paintings in wedding chambers) belongs specifically to women. Kalighat painters called Patuas come from Hindu and Muslim backgrounds. These paintings are generally narrative in nature, depicting one or more scenes from widely prevalent or local Hindu myths. But artists often weave in their own interpretations, their local flora and fauna, and sometimes even their social realities into them. Many of them are now getting into international markets, blurring the lines between the sacred and the secular.

PERFORMING ARTS

As a form of prayer, performing arts have been vitally important in the Hindu tradition since antiquity. In *Sāma* Veda (SV), composed around 1200 BCE, hymns of RV are set to melodies and mentions of early instruments are found. The musical octave of Indian classical music is understood to have its origins here. The Vedic texts also contain references to actors and theater. But since the composition of Bharatmuni's *Nāṭyaśāstra* (between 200 BCE and 200 CE), a comprehensive treatise on performing arts including a theory of aesthetic experience, continuous traditions of dance, music, and theater are traceable. The first chapter of the *Nāṭyaśāstra* contains a narrative about the origins of performing arts. It states that the performing arts were created by the divine creator Brahma as the fifth Veda drawing from the other four. But unlike those, he made it accessible to all including Shudras. This Veda encompasses art, knowledge, yoga, and action; and is meant to offer peace, happiness, and entertainment with representation of diverse emotions. The *Nāṭyaśāstra* has sections on poetry, drama, music, and dance, which have formed foundations of most classical performing arts of India, and embodied expressions of *bhakti*. One of the most original contributions of this text is its exposition of how a performance on stage transports its enjoyer to an imaginative space where she/he experiences human emotions in pure forms and gets transformed morally and spiritually. Thus, performing art is not only a means for praying to the divine, but is seen also as to have an intrinsic power to transform. The stage, therefore, is a sacred space. This understanding has taken such deep cultural roots that performing artists in India, Hindu, or non-Hindu, always make a gesture of reverence to the stage before entering it.

Dance

A distinctive Hindu sacred art form, which has used the *Nāṭyaśāstra* as the foundation, is dance in temple ritual contexts. As grand temples were built with dancing figures carved on walls, dance developed as an integral part of *pūjā* in many parts of India. Over time, various styles of dance developed in various parts of the country. Extensively trained professional dancers – who came to be known as god's servants or wives (*devadāsīs*) – began to be employed for these. These women were exploited by men with power; but their art was considered sacred. The *devadāsī* tradition was prohibited during the British colonial period as debased. But with the efforts of dancers like Rukminidevi Arundale, sacred dances have now been revived with modifications as classical dance forms of India. Several regional styles of classical dance – Bharatnatyam (Tamil Nadu), Kuchipudi (Andhra), Odissi (Orissa), Mohiniyattam and Kathakali (Kerala), Manipuri (Manipur), Kathak (north India), Sattariya (Assam) – are today performed on stages outside of temples, and not as rituals. But all dance forms retain their association with spiritual dimensions of performance and with Hindu mythology, which is woven into the fabric of life in a myriad of ways for Hindus. Major temples also organize dance festivals. These are the aspirational destinations for classical dancers.

While classical dance requiring extensive training remains a highly valued elite art, sacred dances of popular nature abound in all parts of India. These dances use upbeat music and easy dance movements and are accessible to all members of communities. They are not necessarily performed in temples, do not require priestly presence or adhering to ritual purity prescriptions. Most of these are associated with specific festivals or life cycle rituals. Women and men often dance in the open near ritual spaces where the festival images of deities are installed. Some examples of these are: *garbā* (goddess festival) of Gujarat, *rāslila* (Krishna related) of Uttar Pradesh, *theyyam* (for goddess Kali) of Kerala, *sohar* (childbirth) of Bihar/Jharkhand, *giddhā* (various festivities) of Punjab, and *dhunuchi* (goddess festival) of Bengal.

Music

Like dance, Indian classical music traces its origins back to the Vedic literature, especially melodic chants contained in SV. Along with chants, important spiritual concepts also became associated with sound and music in ancient texts. The two most important among them are: (a) *śabda/nād brahman* (sound as the Supreme reality) represented by "Aum" (ॐ); and (b) *nād* (sound) in audible *āhat* (struck) and inaudible *anāhat* (unstruck) forms. As per the first concept, the creation emerged from the vibrations of Brahman as sound, which is represented by Aum (also called Pranava) and forms a part of all Hindu sacred chanting. It is understood to lead one to realize one's connection to the universe. This sound can also be heard in the chants of other religious traditions of the subcontinent such as Jainism, Tibetan Buddhism, and Sikhism. As per the second concept, audible sound is *āhat nād*, produced by contact of two elements/things; and the sound that is subtle and pervasive in the form of cosmic vibrations is unstuck sound (*anāhat nād*). Musical sound as *āhat nād* is viewed as a means of spiritual development. It is thought to be a means to reach the *anāhat* in a higher state of consciousness, pursued by mystics. These ideas are intrinsic to two branches of the elite classical music tradition – north Indian Hindustani (which integrated elements from Persian music during the second millennium) and Carnatic music of south India. But they are also woven in popular regional traditions of sacred music in all strata of the Hindu society. Reference to *āhat* and *anāhat* are found recurrently in vernacular devotional songs, especially in those dedicated to the inner divine.

Hymn and instrumental compositions in classical music styles form parts of liturgy in prominent temples and sects. Each temple or sect has its own substyle. Musicians in these contexts are well trained in the specific style. But for average Hindus, it is devotional songs of regional saint-poets that form their main musical channel for expressing devotion. Two terms widely used for regional devotional songs are *bhajan* and *kīrtan*. The former generally refers to a devotional song sung in solo or chorus, and the latter to formal chorus singing in a call and response manner. These may be in praise of a deity or focused on inner search (Figure 5.4).

Within these broad categories, there are regional variations using popular folk melodies. The songs of Marathi speaking Warkaris we met in the introduction are *abhanga*s. In Karanataka, songs of Shaivite saints called *vachana*s are set in distinct tunes. In Gujarat, hymns called *prabhātiyā* (hymns of dawn) are sung in a soothing melody early in the morning.

Bhajan singers consider it a form of meditation. Yet scholars have shown that in modern times, the popularity of *bhajan* singing events

Figure 5.4 Group singing a hymn to the goddess at home during Navaratri.
Photograph by author.

also creates specific publics, often utilized for political ends and commercial gains. The significance of *bhajan* has been well recognized by scholars of Hinduism. However, an important area of popular religious music that awaits greater attention is women's songs in life cycle rituals and lullabies with mythological themes because these genres are closely linked to important phases in individuals' lives. In lullabies, a major theme remains Rama or Krishna's childhood. A mother singing a lullaby is also educating her child in religious narratives. In wedding songs, the bride and groom are referred to as Rama-Sita, Shiva-Parvati, or Krishna-Radha. As an Indian scholar observed, these songs enhance the meaning of ordinary lives, at least momentarily, by associating them with beloved divine figures.

The above survey indicates that while elite forms of visual and performing arts remain more closely linked to foundational Sanskrit texts, their popular forms give people greater religious agency. They are different in terms of required training and ways of articulation. Yet they have a great deal of overlap and prevail in the same cultural ethos as channels for religious expression. People engage with them in different contexts and for different ends.

AGENCY, AUTHENTICITY, AUTHORITY, DIVERSITY

All religious traditions have practices that serve to filter its core beliefs to followers in an orchestrated manner. The above overview of Hindu religious activities shows that there is an almost overwhelming multiplicity of them. It highlights that in Hinduism, religious agency is intricately layered. It also indicates that people from all strata of the society have channels for authentic religious experience, even though many do not have access to authoritative texts. It is important to note that in the processes through which such a multilayered religious ethos evolved, encounters with regional and even non-Hindu cultures have played key roles. As we have seen, worship of regional deities with specific local elements forms a dynamic part of this ethos; some of the most exquisite paintings of Radha and Krishna have elements influenced by painting style developed at Mughal courts. "Low caste," tribal, and Muslim craftsmen and artists contribute significantly to materials and practices related to festivals. Conversely, elements found in Hindu worship such as offering of flowers are also found at tombs of Sufi saints. The vernacular hymns sung in Hindu, Sufi, and Sikh contexts also share several poetic and musical elements. Over centuries, a culture of mutual exchanges has enriched the religious landscape of India. Following Hinduism with practices rooted exclusively in the ancient Sanskrit sacred texts is immensely difficult if not impossible. The vibrancy of Hindu religious life derives from its multilayered and diversity integrating aspects. Most Hindus are aware of the multiple layers of practices in their tradition – some elite with an aura of authority, and some indigenous and popular. But they do not see them as fragmented pieces of their tradition without connections. They see elite and popular practices to be on a continuum.

Table 5.1 Important terms (for almost all of these, videos are available on YouTube

Traditional term	Meaning
murti	Image
pūjā	Ritual worship
mandir/devālaya	Temple
garbhagṛha	Inner chamber
āratī	Waving of lamps
darśan	Sacred viewing
tīrtha	River ford, pilgrimage site
nād	Sound
āhat/anāhat	Stuck/unstruck
jāp	Repetition of a chant
bhajan	Devotional song
sevā	Service
dāna	Gift giving
Diwali	Festival of light
saṃskāra	Rite of passage
rasa	Nectar. aesthetic delight
sthapati	Sculptor
devadāsī	Temple dancer

FURTHER EXPLORATION SUGGESTIONS

Dehejia, Vidya. 2011. *Indian Art*. London: Phaidon.

Eck, Diana L. 2012. *India: A Sacred Geography*. New York, NY: Harmony Books.

Government of India. "Events and Festivals" and "Art and Culture" on Utsav Portal. Accessed July 25, 2022.
a) https://utsav.gov.in/events-festivals
b) https://utsav.gov.in/event-category/art-culture

Huyler, Stephen P., and Thomas Moore. 1999. *Meeting God: Elements of Hindu Devotion*. New Haven, CT: Yale University Press.

Sahapedia. 2018. "Performing Arts." Accessed July 24, 2022. https://www.sahapedia.org/domains/performing-arts.

Sinha, Laksmi. 1999. *Hindu Saṃskāra*, 1st ed. Delhi: Eastern Book Linkers.

Sree Padma. Ed. 2017. *Inventing and Reinventing the Goddess: Contemporary Iterations of Hindu Deities on the Move*. Lanham, MD: Lexington Books.

EMBRACING MODERNITY

In considering the basics of Hinduism, we have consistently kept in view how religious concepts and practices with deep historical roots change with time. Yet this book does not follow a historical model. The question then arises as to why is the modern period given a separate chapter? There are two reasons for this. First, to understand the Hindu religious life as it prevails today, looking at the developments closer to our times is helpful. And second, in many parts of the world, dramatic changes in the nature of public life during modern times have significantly influenced the religious life of people including Hindus. Hinduism has seen noticeable shifts in beliefs, practices, and sociocultural dynamics in the context of modernity. In this chapter we will consider some important ones. But what is modernity, when did it begin? Modernity is generally thought to begin in the sixteenth century during the European renaissance with the rising prominence of reason and to reach a new height in the nineteenth century with advances in technology and mass media. It has been likened to a muddle or Sphinx by leading historians because the term is seen as Eurocentric and implying a value judgment. Yet it is a broadly useful term for us since the periods covered by it – called "early modern" and "classical modern" – mark important turning points in the history of Hinduism.

DOI: 10.4324/9781315303352-7

In the early modern period, under the prominence of the Mughal empire, Hinduism in India saw acute challenges at times. But it was also a period of growth and creative exchanges. The period saw creation of a composite popular culture with use of shared themes and motifs in religious poetry (in vernacular), art/ architecture, and music by Hindus, Muslims, Sikhs, and Jains. The popularity of these sacred art forms, especially performing arts, has endured through the centuries and people are still able to appreciate them across religious boundaries. The early modern period also saw a proliferation of Hindu sects focused on divinities (especially Rama and Krishna) or saints (Ravidas, Kabir) in north India around the seat of the Mughal empire. These sects were developed by diverse schools of theology. They did not arise expressly in response to external challenges. It was a period of prosperity. Europeans were just entering the Indian market. Wealthy patrons and at times royal courts patronized Hindu religious institutions and temples. Major players within this ethos like emperor Akbar who saw it as a "crowded bazaar of religious ideas" (historian André Wink's expression) were closely familiar with diverse traditions within it. In the classical modern period, Hinduism encountered modernity largely in the context of colonization by the British who were hardly familiar with the cultures and religious ethos of India. Several developments within Hinduism during this period came as Hindus' responses to their tradition's representations in European public discourses. These portrayals ranged from romanticized appreciative interpretations of Sanskrit sacred texts to devastatingly pejorative portrayals of everything Hindu or patronizing depictions of a savage society in the need of civilizing through colonization.

HINDUISM AND EUROPEAN PRESENCE IN INDIA (SEVENTEENTH TO NINETEENTH CENTURIES)

CHANGING CONTEXTS

Close encounters of Hindus with Europeans had begun in the sixteenth and the seventeenth centuries with the establishment of

Portuguese territories in Goa and the arrival of Jesuit missionaries like Roberto de Nobili in South India. While the experience of the former was brutal, the latter opened respectful conversations, even though with missionary goals. By the late eighteenth century, Europeans were competing for political power in Indian territories. The rivals were basically trading companies – British East India Co. (EIC), French East India Co., etc. – that first developed armies and then began developing political control over various parts of India. Of these, EIC emerged the winner with control over large territories. The trading companies did not have much interest in religious matters. With the support of the British parliament, EIC kept missionaries at bay as long as they could, even though some like Warren Hastings (the first Governor General of India under EIC) proposed study of Indian culture and religion for better governance and supported scholars like Sir William Jones who studied Sanskrit texts with local pundits.

In the eighteenth and early nineteenth centuries, translations of Sanskrit sacred texts like the Upanishads and the *Gita* were greatly admired with an element of romanticization by leading intellectuals of Europe like philosopher Arthur Schopenhauer. Yet soon afterwards literal translations of Sanskrit texts like Manu's text on *dharma*, interpreted as "laws," made them into unalterable pillars of a coherent religious system. It was an over-simplified representation of the multilayered, flexible, and diverse religious ethos we have been exploring. In 1813, after heated debates in the British parliament, Christian missionaries won the right to establish missions in India. Already, missionaries were active in Serampore within the Danish colony close to the British capital Calcutta. In contrast to the earlier romanticized portrayals, many representations of "Hinduism" from these quarters were squarely negative, often describing it as the most impure and bloody system with strange multiple gods. In these, ritual worship of images of a host of deities, caste, and status of women received extensive attention. These writings also influenced media depictions of Hinduism in the West garnering greater support for the empire and the missionaries. Such representations can be seen as examples of what Edward Said famously termed "orientalism" – representation of an oriental (Asian, African,

Middle Eastern) culture based on a presumption of the superior-ity of the West.

From the turn of the nineteenth century, education became a major colonial and missionary enterprise. Several missionary schools opened in various parts of British India. While evangelical in orientation, many of them made education accessible for the underprivileged from diverse caste and religious backgrounds. Institutions of higher education were also established in British and other colonies including Serampore and Calcutta. Many young Hindu men in urban areas attended them. A number of them were drawn to European literature, thought and achievements in sci-ence. Some others came in close contacts with missionaries and the expanding colonial administration. Most of them agreed with the colonial/missionary critique of the social issues and many also accepted monotheism as superior to worshiping a pantheon of dei-ties. An intense internal churning led Hindu leaders to search for ways to reform their society and revitalize their tradition. It was in this context that Hinduism's encounter with modernity took momentum.

By the mid-point of the nineteenth century, EIC had acquired control over vast territories. The Mughal emperor retained his crown; but was under British protection with little power. The unrest among rulers whose territories were annexed (often trickily) to EIC colonies and many disgruntled Indian soldiers in the company's army led a revolt against it. The revolt was effectively suppressed. Yet the loss of life of Britishers (including women) was so devastating that the British crown took over the rule of India from EIC in 1858. The rule of the crown, which lasted until 1947, proved more stable with gradual increase in the par-ticipation of the "natives" in governance. Establishment of sev-eral printing presses led to a growth in critical awareness about religious thought and practices and was demonstrated in public debates about them. There was greater confidence in British rule and wider acceptance of rationalist approach to religion with ethical concerns at the core. A few Hindu leaders even spoke of the potential of mutual exchanges between the East and the West. The spirit of reform and revitalization that had been kin-dled in the early nineteenth century continued in the later half too. Yet an acute concern about conversions by missionaries also marked the public debates.

HINDU SOCIO-RELIGIOUS MOVEMENTS (NINETEENTH CENTURY)

The most important development within Hinduism in the nineteenth century was the rise of socio-religious movements. Inevitably, they were immensely diverse. But most of them shared two concerns – reform of the Hindu society and regeneration of Hinduism by reviving what in the view of the movement leaders were its core teachings, lost in the course of history. In the area of reform, getting rid of caste discrimination, especially toward the Dalits, and treatment and status of women remained their main concerns. For revitalization, most movements rejected image worship and sought to retrieve from Hinduism's history elements whose reinterpretation would align with monotheism. Of the scores of leaders and movements that emerged during the period, let us look at a few important ones.

The earliest leader of a Hindu movement was Ram Mohan Roy of Bengal (1772–1833), often called the "father of modern India." Born in a Brahmin family and with early education in Sanskrit and Persian, he was drawn to monotheism. Roy later worked closely with Serampore missionaries and developed a deep affinity for the moral teachings of Jesus Christ. But refusing to accept the supremacy of Christianity, especially of the Trinitarian principle, he first allied with Unitarians and then turned to retrieving Hindu spiritual heritage from the Upanishads, interpreting them as monotheistic. Roy also collaborated with EIC officials for the legal ban of the practice of *satī* (1829) and worked extensively to gain property rights for women. In 1828, he founded Brahmo Sabha (later Brahmo Samaj) with Debendranath Tagore, a society of intellectuals who rejected ritual worship of "idols," worshipped one God, and sought inspiration from ancient Hindu scriptures (especially Upanishads' idea of Brahman) with openness to similar ideas from other traditions. They did not recognize caste. This was the first Hindu society to formally open a direction. Another Brahmin reformer from Bengal, Iswarchandra Vidyasagar (1820–1891), individually pursued the cause of girls' education and widow remarriage. These early reformers worked closely with EIC officials but were often opposed by orthodox Hindus. Their aspirations for the end of gender and caste discrimination were well-meaning. but they came from elite men and not directly from women or lower-caste people.

Voices of the marginalized were heard more clearly in public discourses a few decades later in the western Indian city of Pune where Jyotirao Phule (1827–1890), a rationalist reformer from a "low-caste," worked alongside his wife for women's education and betterment of their lives. He was an outspoken critic of caste discrimination who fought for rights of the low caste/Dalit community members. He had the foresight to see the synergy between the Dalit and women's issues. Like Roy, Phule also worked closely with British officials and missionaries whom he greatly admired. Phule's detailed profile is given in the last section of this chapter.

Two other remarkable developments of the late nineteenth century were: (a) the spread of the Arya Samaj movement founded by the ascetic Swami Dayanand Saraswati (1824–1883) and (b) the visit of another ascetic, Swami Vivekananda (1863–1902) to America, to attend the first Parliament of World Religions (1893). Swami Dayanand, originally from Gujarat, left home early and became a wandering ascetic. Later he developed the opinion that Hinduism had deteriorated from its Vedic origins and its contemporary social evils sprang from this decline. With a resolve to revive what he saw as Hinduism's pure golden age, he founded Arya Samaj (society of nobles) in 1875. His approach was staunchly rational, rejecting image worship, superstitions, child marriage, and hereditary caste with hierarchy (though he recognized it on the basis of mental qualities). Dayanand traveled widely in India and engaged Hindu, Muslim, and Christian clerics in sharp debates, challenging their beliefs and practices. While he shared ideals of social reform with movements like Brahmo Samaj, he was critical of them since he believed that they sought to present moral exemplars from other traditions and overlooked ancient Vedic seers. Dayanand also introduced a practice called *śuddhi* (purification) by which Hindus who had converted to other religions could be reconverted. Some scholars trace elements of the current political Hinduism to his work.

Arya Samaj became extremely successful and widespread in Punjab and north India. It is still an active religious denomination. To this day, it remains the leader in the area of education (especially of girls) outside of the government system. The other Swami, Vivekananda, was the disciple of Bengali mystic Ramakrishna. Vivekananda attended the first Parliament of World Religions in Chicago (1893) as a Hindu representative. His speech, in which he presented Hindu philosophy as based in the teachings of the Upanishads and open to all similar currents of thought, was warmly received. He quickly became popular among Americans who were open to learning from eastern philosophies. He also often spoke about what the East and the West can learn from one another. He founded the Vedanta society in 1894 in New York and in 1900 in California. He dedicated the rest of his short life to the cause of social work and education in the organization in his guru's name – the Ramakrishna Mission – and to revitalize the Hindu tradition.

As the above overview indicates, the nineteenth-century socio-religious movements strove intensely to rid the Hindu society of its problems of injustice with regard to caste and gender and to simultaneously reform the tradition with selected elements from its long history to align it with modernity. Even though the social problems they tried to eradicate still persist to an extent, collectively, leaders and movements of the nineteenth century gave a new direction to Hinduism. Because of the ways in which they responded, the scathing and often exaggerated critique of the tradition by some Europeans, which was humiliating for Hindus, proved beneficial in the end.

NATIONALISM, PARTITION, AND THEREAFTER (TWENTIETH AND TWENTY-FIRST CENTURIES)

EARLY TWENTIETH CENTURY – PATRIOTISM AND COMMUNALISM

If the nineteenth century was a century of socio-religious reforms, in the twentieth century, religion in public life became closely intertwined with politics. Tensions between the two numerically largest religious communities in India – Hindus and Muslims –

which had started building in the late nineteenth century, began to turn into conflicts, often violent. It was not that in pre-British India, there were no skirmishes. At times, tensions did arise; but they could be more easily contained with courtly interventions under Hindu or Muslim rulers who closely knew the ethos. In the 1857 revolt, Hindu and Muslim soldiers and commanders/rulers had fought the EIC army together. But in the second half of the nineteenth century, as British rule stabilized, the cooperation turned first into rivalry and later into suspicion among some powerful groups in both communities. It remains a matter of debate whether the British purposefully employed a policy of "divide and rule" to retain their supremacy. But some British actions and policies did intensify the feelings of distrust. Inclusion of the criterion of religion in the census conducted from 1872 onwards formally highlighted the significance of religious identity as an aspect of citizenship, even as greater opportunities for natives opened in the government infrastructure. The partition of Bengal (Hindu majority West Bengal and Muslim majority East Bengal) in 1905 was purported to be for administrative purposes. But the then Viceroy of India, Lord Curzon, made references to their religious makeup underscoring the differences.

The tensions steadily accelerated. The Indian National Congress, founded as a secular political organization of Indians in 1885, was not able to win the confidence of Muslims who had felt sidelined. Politically active Muslims founded the Muslim League in 1906. In 1915, Hindu Mahasabha was established as an organization, which became a political party in 1933. With these, the chasm in political interests of the two communities kept widening. Communal riots marked by violence began to occur repeatedly. It was also a time when several nationalist movements for freedom from the British had gained momentum. Congress, under the leadership of Gandhi during the 1920s and 1930s, had garnered tremendous popular support with participation of women and men of all backgrounds in large numbers. But gradually a demand was made by the Muslim League that British India should be partitioned into two nations on religious grounds if it became independent. The partition of British India into Hindu majority India and Muslim majority Pakistan (on its east and west sides) did occur at the time of independence in 1947. Freedom from

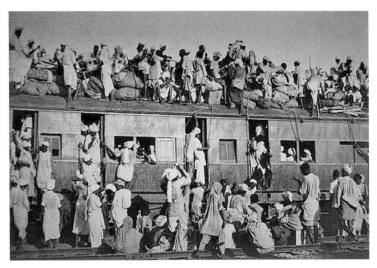

Figure 6.1 Partition of Punjab, India 1947, migration.
Source: Wikimedia Commons.
Photographer: Unknown

the British came with the incalculable cost of human life. The massacre of people on both sides of the newly created borders remains unprecedented in human history. Mobs from Hindu, Muslim, and Sikh communities attacked one another out of frustration and anger caused by their displacement from homelands. Millions migrated from one side to the other in a state of hopelessness (Figure 6.1).

The tragic implications of the partition are still unfolding, often with violence based in religious identity politics or extremism.

AFTER PARTITION

India chose to be a secular democracy at the time of independence. A considerable percentage of its population remains committed to the ideal of secularism with respect for all religions. However, more recently, events at some contested sites for which both Hindu and Muslim communities have attachment because of religious and/or historical reasons have led to controversies and in some cases, violent conflicts termed "communal riots." In these, both communities suffer. Yet being a minority in India, Muslims are often at the receiving end. In such conflicts, old wounds resurface at the intersections of faith, history, and identity politics. Quite apart from riots, in some circles that actually oppose violence, advocacy is still heard for a Hindu Rashtra (Hindu nation), an ideology of religious nationalism known as Hindutva. Some proponents of this ideology doubt the loyalty (to the nation state) of Muslims, for whom too India has been the dear homeland for centuries. Hindus on the other side of the border/s (former east Pakistan is now Bangladesh), who form much smaller minorities in their countries, live in analogous situations. They too live in a state of vulnerability to violence in their ancestral lands. In the former British colonies in South Asia including Sri Lanka, with the prevalence of identity politics post independence, religious minorities face a similar predicament. However, after over 70 years of independence in all these parts, the role of British rule in the rise of this situation is debatable. The situation arises out of complex issues rooted in feelings of historical injustice that await solutions through skillful and sensitive cultural as well as political engagement locally and internationally. The issues related to identity politics are not basics of Hinduism as a religious tradition. But being aware of them helps understand the news about them, which appear in the national, international, and social media rather prominently.

Two other themes that also figure prominently in public discourses and media are discrimination against the Dalits and position of women in the Hindu society. These two themes have retained media attention since the nineteenth century. In the area of caste discrimination since the time of Jyotirao Phule, several Dalit leaders have made significant contributions to the upliftment of lower-caste and former untouchable communities. The most important among them was Dr. B.R. Ambedkar (1891–1956), a prominent public figure and intellectual whose work spanned several decades of the twentieth century. Born in a Dalit family as Bhimrao Sakpal, he was given the last name Ambedkar by a Brahmin school teacher of that name. Ambedkar went on to earn a doctoral degree in economics from Columbia University, New York, and D.Sc. from the London School of Economics. Still, he experienced humiliating discrimination recurrently on his return to India and spent the rest of his life fighting for the rights of "untouchables." Toward the end of his life, he converted to Buddhism along with his followers. Ambedkar, like Phule, worked closely with the British and held high offices in their administration. In independent India, he served as the chairman of the constitution drafting committee, which incorporated several key affirmative action measures for the Dalits. This has made a positive difference in the fields of education and government employment for them to a degree. A number of upper-caste Hindus acknowledge the historical injustice done to the Dalits and make efforts to correct it. Yet, as mentioned a few times earlier, the goal of equality remains far from achieved. The Dalits still face discrimination and at times violence. Women in all layers of the society have made tremendous strides in work forces in formal and informal sectors. They have been prominent figures in local and national politics including the Prime Minister (Indira Gandhi) and Presidents (Pratibha Patil, Draupadi Murmu) of the country. With prolonged efforts of women activists, Hindu women have gained equal rights to property as daughters and wives. They are also getting considerable respect as priests and gurus. There is gradual acceptance of gender fluidity as well. However, complete gender equality is still a dream, especially in the areas of leadership positions in business and other professional fields as well as in household chores. While issues persist, it needs to be noted that in the context of modernity, there has been incremental yet definitive progress toward retributive justice in the Hindu society through processes of negotiations and accommodations, and thanks to many actors in history including the British.

FAITH PRACTICES IN THE ERA OF GLOBALIZATION

Because religion related topics with social and political implications generally receive more coverage in both commercial and social media in most parts of the world, developments in the area of faith practices receive less attention. For Hinduism the topics getting most attention are caste, gender, and religious nationalism. But equally fascinating are transformations of faith practices brought about by global market economy, technological advances, and growing stress on individual choice. Global market developments propelled by technology have been influencing practices of all religious communities around the world in recent times. Like all other aspects of life, the arrival of the internet platforms, and social media have deeply influenced religion. As sociologist Peter Berger has argued, even though religion has continued to thrive as a social force disproving the earlier predictions of its gradual disappearance in the modern age, the way it is practiced today has shifted considerably from its traditional forms. This is amply demonstrated in contemporary Hinduism. While Hindu practices discussed earlier still thrive dynamically, their forms have changed and new layers have been added to them in the virtual space. Some modifications are related to economic advance while some address the contemporary global concerns for social justice, individual freedom, environment protection, and stress management. Let us look at the innovative dimensions of a few important components of Hinduism – religious philosophy and guidance for life, as well as practices such as festival rituals, pilgrimage, life cycle performances, and sacred arts. These dimensions are copiously reflected on related websites and are analogous to developments in many religious traditions.

In the area of religious teachings, locally and internationally known spiritual teachers including leaders of sects incorporate two things: (a) focus on the subjective (individual) side of devotion and personal transformation rather than simply glorification of the divine or the guru and (b) aspects of social responsibility and service. Inner transformation through devotion and practices like meditation has been a part of Hindu spiritual traditions for millennia. But its articulation now is also linked often to professional efficiency and mental well-being. Similarly, *sevā* has been an important value for Hindus for centuries as we saw earlier. But today it is stressed as a part of activities of religious organizations/fellowships. Further, in view of many individuals leaning toward the spiritual rather than the religious, some Hindu leaders define their organizations in terms of the former and do not even mention the term "Hindu" on the front page of their sites, even though their practices such as chants, etc. mention Hindu deities and their mottos often draw from peace mantras of Vedic literature. These leaders are rearticulating Hindu spirituality for the twenty-first century. The profile of a contemporary woman guru, Amritanandamayi, is included in the last section. Links for a few websites are also given for further exploration.

In recent years, an important area in which Hindu leaders are striving to make a contribution in collaboration with other leaders is the environment. Directing attention to the components of Hinduism that present nature as sacred, suggest a continuum between human life and nature, stress human responsibility in maintaining the harmony in the cosmos, and recognize *karma* at a collective level, they advocate for environment friendly choices. In 2009, a Hindu Declaration on Climate Change was made at the Parliament of World Religions. Even though some locales and rivers in India that are considered important parts of Hindu sacred geography are facing critical environmental issues, there is gradual growth in awareness about the resources for environment protection within the tradition.

Among religious practices and sacred arts, the most observable change is construction of grand temples and retreat centers (*āśrams*) in several parts of the world. Spread on large premises, with towers or stories visible from a distance, they attract thousands of visitors (not necessarily devotees) every year. Some observers see such temples within India as markers of religious nationalism. However, the people who take pride in them, view them as indicators of the community's growing prosperity. For those who grew up in India when it was generally referenced for its poverty, it is an achievement. The trusts of several major temples upload videos of their *pūjā* on their websites and on platforms like Youtube for *darśan*. Most also have tabs for offerings (donation). As mentioned earlier, trusts at pilgrimage centers have also developed them as tourism sites with easy transportation and comfortable accommodation options, attracting large numbers of pilgrims.

Similar influence of financial growth is also seen in magnificence of *pujā*s at major temples, pilgrimage sites, and enthusiastic public festival celebrations in which people from all sectors of the society participate. Festivals are celebrated with a lot of fanfare with people spending more money on sweets, clothing, gifts, parties, and decorations. The religious meaning often recedes in the background during celebration, even though newspapers carry full stories about them. As I have discussed in my essay on Gujarat's *garbā* dance during the goddess festival Navaratri in contemporary times, paradoxically, the divinities are both present and absent in the festivities. In celebrations animated by consumerism and boosted by business ventures, the lines between the sacred and the secular are blurred. This blurring draws younger generations to festivals. But some public intellectuals find the celebrations being taken over by businesses disconcerting. They suggest that in this, the significance of family gatherings and roles of women are compromised. Yet the blurring makes possible the participation of people from diverse backgrounds (often non-Hindus) as providers of goods and services for festivals. During Navaratri, some of the most sought after singers of *garbā* songs in Gujarat are Muslims. The technological advances also allow family members far from one another to gather online and celebrate festivals together thousands of miles apart. These new layers added by global businesses and technological advances are generally welcomed by Hindus.

From their early homes in north-west India in antiquity, Hindu divinities and their devotees have indeed traveled long distances in time and space, including the virtual one. The journey has been turbulent at times and people have faltered in their steps and moral judgment. But the tradition has continued to flow in modernity and post-modernity. In this journey, some social and religious leaders have played important roles by offering spiritual guidance to people at home and internationally or by boldly pointing out the wrongs prevalent in their society. Before we end our overview of Hinduism in the modern period with a recent scene in Mumbai, let us look at brief biographical sketches of three Hindu leaders who belong to three different periods discussed above. Each one's life and work combine elements of the paths of *karma*, *bhakti*, and *jnāna* in different ways.

A NINETEENTH-CENTURY MAHATMA, JYOTIRAO PHULE (1827–1890)

For millions in the world, the term "Mahatma" (great soul) brings to mind the figure of Mohandas K. Gandhi, who was given the title in 1915 by another great personality, poet Rabindranath Tagore. But not many people globally know that the title had been given 27 years earlier to Jyotirao Phule, a social reformer from Maharashtra and an early proponent in women's education along with his wife Savitri Phule. Born in Pune in a family of gardeners, Māli, considered low in the caste hierarchy, he attended Scottish Missionary High School. As a young man, he had a chance to visit schools for girls/women (who had no access to education in that era) established by the missionaries. Impressed by the educational opportunities offered by them to the marginalized, Phule remained a lifelong admirer of Europeans and considered British rule a great advantage to India. He gradually became a successful government contractor and entrepreneur in Pune and was also appointed a commissioner on the municipal council of the city.

Phule was married at 13 to a girl from his own caste – Savitri. When Phule was 18, a humiliating experience of discrimination at a Brahmin friend's wedding led him to become sharply critical of the caste system. He developed a view that Aryans, who were ancestors of Brahmins, had invaded India and subjugated the original inhabitants of the land by placing them the lowest in the caste hierarchy or even outside of it as "untouchables." He was scathingly critical of Vedic texts and even the *Ramayana*, which he saw as sources for caste oppression. In addition to lower castes and untouchables, Phule saw women as victims of Brahminical supremacy, which he decided to resist. He first educated his wife Savitribai; and then in partnership with her, opened several institutions for women's education in Pune. The couple also opened schools for Dalit children, who were not allowed in schools. In another surprisingly liberal move, they established a shelter for widows who became mothers. This institution was open to all women, but was particularly beneficial to high-caste widows, who, as we have seen, were not allowed to remarry.

Phule later founded "Satyashodhak Samaj" (society in the search of truth) with a rationalist approach. The organization had members from diverse religious and caste groups including Brahmins. They opposed image worship like other reformer groups. But their main focus was on the rights of the groups they identified as marginalized. Even though working alongside Brahmins in his organization, Phule opposed their appointments as teachers in schools. He even declined an invitation to attend the meeting of the Marathi literary society because he saw it as representing Brahmin ideology and interests. Because of Phule's uncompromising approach in efforts to reform his society, he is described as a "radical reformer" in *Sources of Indian Traditions*, Vol. 2. It is noteworthy that despite being a staunch rationalist and a harsh critic of the caste system, Phule did not convert to Christianity or Buddhism like some later leaders from lower castes, notably Ambedkar. He also saw *bhakti* saint-poets of Maharashtra like Tukaram (about whom we heard in the Introduction) as sources of inspiration. Phule's recognition of affinity among low-caste communities and women, and his fearless resistance to social injustice can be seen as his significant contributions to Hinduism. He was among the first to articulate the pain inflicted by caste discrimination from the point of view of its victims. For this, another reformer from Bombay bestowed on him the title of Mahatma in 1888. Today, Phule's legacy endures in several educational institutions for the marginalized in Maharashtra. A statue of him was unveiled in 2003 by the prime minister of the country in front of the parliament house in the capital, Delhi. The most fitting tribute to the work of the Phule couple is, however, seen in the renaming of the University of Pune as Savitribai Phule University. The institution's official song stresses combining knowledge (*jnāna*) with just *karma* and the *bhakti* qualities of the heart.

AN EARLY TEACHER OF YOGA IN AMERICA, PARAMHANSA YOGANANDA (1893–1952)

Paramhansa Yogananda, the first eminent yoga teacher to settle in the USA, was born in a Kayastha (upper caste) family in

Gorakhpur in north India as Mukund Lal Ghosh. Since child-hood, Mukund was in search of a true spiritual guru, whom he found in Swami Yukteshwar Giri, an eminent guru of Kriya Yoga in the nineteenth century. Swami Yukteshwar had come in contact with missionaries in India. He was a liberal intellectual with an open mind and wrote comparatively on the Vedas and the Bible. Yukteshwar trained Mukund extensively in yoga and also allowed him to choose his spiritual name Yogananda. Young Yogananda first opened a school in West Bengal, which com-bined instruction of yoga with modern secular education. In 1920, 17 years after Swami Vivekananda's first tour in America, Yogananda was invited by American Unitarians for a convention in Boston. With the blessings of a great guru of his spiritual lin-eage, Yogananda arrived in the USA and spent the rest of his life (except one long trip) in America.

He made several lecture tours in the early 1920s and estab-lished the center of Self-realization Fellowship in Los Angeles in 1925, attracting thousands including celebrities. His guru Yukteshwar gave him the highest spiritual title for a monk, Paramhansa, during his trip to India in 1935. In 1946, he pub-lished *Autobiography of a Yogi* describing his spiritual journey. The book met with phenomenal success. It has sold over four million copies till date and is considered one of the most influential spir-itual works of the twentieth century, a favorite of American business magnate Steve Jobs. His important teachings based on Kriya Yoga included (a) harmony between Jesus's teachings in Krishna's message about yoga in BG; (b) potential of every per-son to reach divine consciousness through disciplined following of the science of yoga; and (c) uniting science with religion for the betterment of mankind. By the time of his death in 1952, he was a greatly loved spiritual teacher in America and certainly the first to make yoga a spiritual discipline followed by thousands in the country. Today, his followers are found in close to 175 coun-tries in the world at several Self-realization Fellowship centers. In India the fellowship is called Yogoda Satsang. Two commem-orative postal stamps were issued in India to honor Yogananda (1977, 2017). His focus on the shared spirituality of mankind and his stress on yoga as a discipline for cultivation of the human consciousness contributed significantly to gaining respect for Hinduism in the West.

MOTHER (AMMA) OF THOUSANDS, MATA AMRITANANDAMAYI (1953–)

Mata Amritanandamayi, born in Kerala in a fisherman family as Sudhamani in 1953, is a female Hindu guru of international prominence. She is known globally as "the hugging saint" because of her practice of embracing all who come for her *darśan*. For this motherly gesture, she is also called "Amma" by her disciples. Amritanandamayi's spiritual journey did not begin in school or with a guru, but with the chore of collecting scrap food she performed for her family's cattle. At an early age, this led her to come in close contact with the poor and to develop compassion for them, which she began to express through spontaneously hugging them. She also began to compose devotional songs and sing them while performing her chores. Her spiritual journey was that of self-cultivation through compassion. This is also reflected in her own practices as a spiritual mentor.

If the work of Jyotirao Phule and Paramhansa Yogananda, the two male leaders discussed above, were rooted in selfless action and knowledge, respectively, Amritanandamayi's approach is grounded in the heart. She considers *karma*, *bhakti*, and *jñāna* as three pillars of spirituality. But at the heart of her spiritual mentorship is her emotionally reassuring embrace. At times, she sits for 20 hours at a stretch to meet her visitors in this way. Her disciples say that her embrace opens their hearts to cultivation of qualities such as compassion, patience, forgiveness, and restraint. Cultivating these qualities, Amritanandamayi stresses, prepares the mind to approach the Ultimate. With this basic philosophy, she has won thousands of followers over the world to whom she refers as her "children" and not "disciples." Her followers work in a variety of social service projects – related to food, education, disaster relief, environment, women's empowerment, etc. – in different parts of the world in a network of organizations termed "Embracing the World." She has received several honorary degrees and awards for her work from Europe, America, and India. She is the subject of some books and documentaries as well. She is recognized as one of the most influential women spiritual leaders in the world.

In modern history, there have been hundreds of guru figures like the leaders whose lives we considered above. Many have become subjects of controversies in countries where basic expectations from religion are fundamentally different from Hinduism. A few were found fraudulent too. But in general, like the three leaders profiled above, they have been able to establish constructive relationships with people around the world. They have taken advantage of the freedom of interpretation and multivocality in their tradition and brought prestige to it by building communities of people with diverse backgrounds.

A TRIP TO SIDDHIVINAYAK AND A STORY OF FLUIDITY

This short note is added to draw attention to the diverse situations that simultaneously prevail on ground in India. Because of the reports of communal tensions found daily in the media, a peaceful coexistence of diverse communities seems improbable from afar. Yet a recent trip to the famous Siddhivinayak Ganesha temple, and one to the tomb of the Muslim saint Haji Ali in the densely populated city of Mumbai highlighted for me that despite tensions and conflicts, most people find ways to live in harmony with their co-patriots. People from diverse faiths, identifiable from their attires, could be seen at both places considered powerful in fulfilling wishes. Respectful exchanges could be seen at both. Even more recently than these trips, an employee with a Hindu name at an institution I was visiting revealed that for his community in Karnataka, one of their most important festivals is the Shia Muslim festival of Muharram, which they celebrate according to the Islamic calendar. People working in far off towns return home for it. Along with gestures of mutual respect at sacred sites, this kind of fluidity in practice also helps the fabric of a diverse society to remain intact and many hope that it will continue to do so.

Table 6.1 Hinduism Since the Nineteenth Century

Early nineteenth century	• Scathing critique of the tradition in missionary tracks and European media • Ram Mohan Roy's work with early missionaries • Social reform initiatives like the legal ban of *satī* with the support of EIC officials (1829) • Rejection of image worship and rituals in favor of philosophical reflection, and disregard for caste in Brahmo Sabha/Samaj (1828)
Mid to late nineteenth century	• Rule transfer from EIC to the British crown (1858) • Proliferation of socio-religious movement with reform of society and revitalization of Hinduism as the goal • Jyotirao Phule • Arya Samaj of Dayanand Saraswati (1873) • Development of distinct religious identities as aspects of citizenship • Women's education and participation in public life, widow remarriage • Swami Vivekananda in America
Early to mid-twentieth century	• Nationalist Freedom Movements • Participation of multitudes of women and men in the movement/s led by Gandhi • Establishments of Muslim League (1906) and Hindu Mahasabha (1915, 1933) • Increasing tensions between Hindus and Muslims • Independence and the Partition of British India (1947)
Mid-twentieth century present	• India as secular democracy – provisions for the underprivileged in the constitution • Contested sites and communal riots • Hindu religious nationalism • Vulnerability of minorities in former British Colonies in South Asia • Economic growth and technological advances – transformation of religion • Hindu gurus on the international scene

FURTHER EXPLORATION SUGGESTIONS

Babb, Lawrence A., and Susan S. Wadley, Eds. 1995. *Media and the Transformation of Religion in South Asia*. Philadelphia, PA: University of Pennsylvania.

Carson, Penelope. 2012. *The East India Company and Religion, 1698–1858*. Woodbridge, Suffolk: Boydell Press.

Gould, William. 2012. *Religion and Conflict in Modern South Asia*. Cambridge, UK. Cambridge University Press.

McDermott, Rachel Fell. *Sources of Indian Traditions*, 3rd ed. New York, NY: Columbia University Press, 2014.

Public Broadcasting Services. "Hinduism and Modern India." Video. Aired on January 22, 2010. https://www.pbs.org/video/religion-ethics-newsweekly-hinduism-and-modern-india/.

Smith, David. 2003. *Hinduism and Modernity*. Religion in the Modern World. Malden, MA: Blackwell Pub.

WEBSITES

Isha Foundation. 2022. "Isha." Accessed August 4, 2022. https://isha.sadhguru.org/us/en/center/isha-yoga-center-coimbatore.

Mata Amritanandamayi (Amma). 2022. "Embracing the World." Accessed August 4, 2022 https://www.embracingtheworld.org/.

Shri Arasuri Ambaji Mata Devsthan Trust. 2022. "Ambaji Temple." Accessed August 4, 2022. https://www.ambajitemple.in/.

HINDUISM BEYOND INDIA

India inevitably appears as the focus in all works on Hinduism as the land of the historical development of the tradition and also because more than 90% of the world's Hindus live in that country. Yet Hindu communities have prevailed in many other parts of the world – for millennia in some, for centuries in some others, and for decades in a few (https://en.wikipedia.org/wiki/Hinduism_by_country#/media/File:Countries_by_percentage_of_adherents_to_Hinduism.svg). Approximately 100 million Hindus are estimated to live outside of India at present. Their religious life demands attention in any consideration of Hinduism. In this last chapter, we will look at some basic aspects of Hinduism beyond India. The immense diversity found in regional vernacular texts and practices within India is echoed in Hinduism internationally too. However, unlike diversity within India, which is spatially rooted, in the international contexts, varied forms of Hinduism are linked not only to the local cultures but also to the historical contexts of the tradition's arrival in various parts of the world. In our exploration, we will look at both these aspects.

"OTHERS" AND "OUTSIDERS"

Before we begin our exploration of Hinduism outside of India, let us first look at the Hindu view of and interactions with "others"

DOI: 10.4324/9781315303352-8

and "outsiders" in general. This will allow us to briefly review Hindus' relations with the followers of other traditions that have been only passingly referenced earlier. People of the early Vedic culture, as we saw, called themselves Ārya. The term used for non-Aryans (who did not speak Sanskrit) was *mleccha* which originally meant "speaking indistinctly," but later also came to mean "unrefined," "impure," and "outsider." In ancient Hindu, Buddhist, and Jain texts (Sanskrit, Pali and Ardhamgadhi), a *mleccha* was presented as the opposite of an *ārya*, "a noble person of refinement." The terms *ārya* and *mleccha* were parts of common vocabulary among the three traditions, which also shared core concerns such as release from cycles of rebirth, etc. Because of the shared components, there was fluidity among the three traditions in the religious lives of common people. Even with sharp debates among the elites about the ways of achieving the spiritual goal of ultimate freedom as well as rivalry for followers and patronage, for the Vedic people, Jains and Buddhists were *nāstika*s (not believing in the Vedas), "others" to a degree, but not "outsiders." Most royal courts and aristocrats patronized all three traditions in their spheres of influence. The fluidity created by shared aspects allowed people to celebrate common festivals, bond over practices such as worship of trees and spirits, and venerate holy persons of all traditions.

In later periods, Muslims and Christians did fall under the category of "outsiders." Avoiding contact with them in ritual contexts has remained a major concern especially for upper caste Hindus since the early second millennium. Yet first Islam and then in the nineteenth and early twentieth centuries Christianity were the religious traditions of powerful rulers of India. Elite Hindus found ways to work with them in courtly and government settings. They also engaged with high officials to gain benefits for or introduce social reforms in their communities as we have seen. At the popular religion level, fluidity still persisted in practices such as songs of regional saint-poets in various traditions including Sikhism and openness to spaces and communities related to saintly figures (Sufi tombs and Kabir's disciples for example). Hindus in India have continued to venerate saintly figures from other traditions. Generally, this is attributed to popular Hinduism's lack of concern for ritual purity. While this is valid to a considerable extent, an acceptance of

multiple ways to express the experience of the sacred has been integral also to the elite current of Hinduism since the time of *Rig Veda*
(RV), expressed in statements like "Truth is one; sages say it differ-
ently" (RV 1.164.46). There have certainly been instances of conflicts over religious identity in the past few centuries in which
Hindus in India have engaged. But in general, their stance has been
to see other religions as valid paths chosen by others.

BEYOND INDIAN SHORES

Until recent centuries, many Hindus considered it a taboo to travel
to other parts of the world by crossing the oceans. The roots of this
belief are traced to some injunctions of ancient *dharma* texts dated
to the turn of the Common Era. The concern here is that a person
is unable to perform daily rituals and maintain their purity on long
sea routes, which is not the case with land travel. The taboo came
to be expressed in the vernaculars as *kālā pānī* (black waters) and
was observed strictly until the nineteenth century by many Indians
(including Jains for non-violence concerns). Yet, there was generally room for debates and accommodations. In Gandhi's autobiography, there is an interesting account of such a debate. When the
possibility of his traveling to England to study law was discussed
among his family (of Bania trader caste) and friends, his uncle had
concerns not about ritual purity but about maintaining a vegetarian diet. It was the family's Brahmin friend who argued in favor of
going for the sake of career advancement prospects. Finally, after
Gandhi's taking a few vows to his mother's and family's satisfac-
tion, he was able to go. Hindus have indeed traveled to and settled
in far off lands since ancient times, highlighting that *dharma* texts
offered only prescriptions and were not taken as commandments or
laws. In what follows, we will consider dispersion of Hindus and
Hinduism to distant shores in three phases – early centuries of the
Common Era, during the colonial context, and since the late twentieth century. We will consider their four major forms – Hinduism
transmitted and taking roots in lands beyond India, religion of
Hindu migrants, embracing of Hinduism by non-Hindus, and
Hindu cultural influences. Hindus form a majority in two coun-
tries other than India, in others they are a minority. Hindus in
Pakistan and Bangladesh form a special category because even

though outside of the present-day India, they did not migrate there. They live as minorities in their ancestral lands.

EARLY TRANSMISSION OF HINDUISM (FIRST MILLENNIUM)

South Asia

Nepal: The country with the highest percentage of Hindu population (81% approximately) in the world, Nepal, is also a land that forms an important section of the northern boundary of Hinduism in the Himalayas where the tradition has taken deep roots. As per a myth found locally and in some Sanskrit Puranas, a sage named "Ne" performed intense asceticism in the region and became its protector. Therefore, it came to be known as "Nepal" (protected by Ne). It is also a region in which the Buddha was born. Buddhist monuments appeared in Nepal before the Common Era. But from its early centuries, Buddhism and Hinduism have formed key components of the religious life in the region, indistinguishable from each other in some respects. During the period of Licchavi kings (fifth through the eighth centuries) along with Buddhist monuments, the famous Shiva temple of Pashupatinath was constructed. Historically, while some ceremonies and sacred spaces are clearly demarcated as one or the other, in many, Hindu and Buddhist images are found together, often on the same panel. During my 2018 trip to the country, I was struck by the difference between the matter-of-fact manner in which Nepalis worshipped the images standing together at various sites and non-Nepalis talking about them as "Hindu" or "Buddhist."

A major thread linking the two traditions in Nepal is Tantra, a set of non-Vedic spiritual texts and practices for inner transformation, using physical postures, material elements, geometric designs, and meditative techniques such as visualization and absorption of sound vibrations. In Hinduism, Tantra influences began to be seen in the worship of deities (Shiva, the goddess, and Vishnu) during the Puranic period. Even the core components of Hinduism such as *pūjā* and temple designs are deeply influenced by Tantra. Especially strong links to Tantra are found in Shaivite asceticism and worship of goddesses, both of which have robust presence in Kashmir and Himalayan regions including Nepal (Figure 7.1).

Figure 7.1 Hindu sacred places in Kathmandu valley Nepal. Left: Vishnu on Serpent Shesha. Middle: Temple with Pagoda style tower. Right: Image Kal Bhairva form of Shiva in a City Square.

Photograph by author.

In Buddhism, Tantra is at the core of the Vajrayana branch, prevalent in Tibet, Nepal, Bhutan – the Himalayan regions in general. In both Hinduism and Buddhism, in the visual arts influenced by Tantra, celestial beings are represented in their dual gracious and terrifying forms, often in geometric designs called *yantra* or *maṇḍala*. In these, aspects of locally worshipped nature spirits and Hindu or Buddhist deities are synthesized. According to one interpretation, the entire country/region of Nepal is a *maṇḍala*. Hinduism and Buddhism thrive within it as intertwined traditions.

Because of Nepal's permeable boundaries with India, Hinduism there shares many features with its north Indian forms. But a few Nepalese Hindu practices, especially of the Kathmandu valley, are distinctive if not unique. These include worship of Bhairava (Shiva's powerful and often terrifying form), Kumari (a pre-puberty young girl seen as Durga's temporary manifestation), and Indra (the Vedic deity) as well as the festival of Dassain (goddess festival Navaratri in India). All of these draw elements from haloed Sanskrit texts (like the *Devi Mahātmya* extolling Durga). However, these are sewn with Tantric aspects, local myths, worship practices that involve alcohol and meat, material culture, and season cycles, which ground them firmly in the land.

Sri Lanka: Another land outside of India where Hinduism has deep roots is Sri Lanka. Here, worship of Shiva prevailed as a major religious current integrated with local animistic practices even before the arrival of Buddhism in the third-century BCE. Indeed, in the *Ramayana*, Sri Lanka is identified as the territory of Ravana, a devout worshipper of Shiva. Even today, among Sri Lankan Hindus, Shiva worship forms a major core of religious life. Since Sri Lankan Hindus have closest ties to Tamil Nadu, their practices have close parallels with Shaivite traditions in south India, especially that of Shaiva Siddhanta. In addition to Shiva, two other prominent celestial figures related to Sri Lanka that appear in Hindu myths are Yakshas (nature spirits), and their king Kubera (deity of wealth), believed to be the king of Sri Lanka before Ravana who provide the deepest layer of religious life on the island. Their images are found engraved even on Buddhist sacred monuments throughout Sri Lanka. Images of Hindu gods and goddesses are also found in antechambers of Buddhist temples, indicating their prevalence as another layer.

The coexistence of Hindu and Buddhist worship practices is seen here too, but not as closely tied. They are sometimes in harmony and sometimes in tension. Of particular interest is the annual festival of Esela Perehera at a sacred site called Kataragama in south-eastern Sri Lanka (https://www.youtube.com/watch?v=GRYOS7FPEZU), which, according to scholars, belonged originally to local people called Veddas. Over the centuries, it became sacred for several religious communities. The site now has Buddhist (Katargama deviyo) and Hindu (Murugan) shrines as well as tombs of Muslim holy men. In recent times it has been attracting large groups of pilgrims during the festival in July/August. While tensions due to contested claims among the traditions surface at times, what unites pilgrims from diverse backgrounds is the cluster of rituals such as Kawadi dancing and fire walking that belonged originally to the Veddas, who still remain in charge.

South-East Asia

Further transmission of Hinduism outside of India occurred through traders and emissaries in the early centuries of the Common Era during the reign of the powerful Cholas in South India. Hindu religion and cultural influences traveled to South-East Asian regions including the present-day Cambodia and Indonesia where they took deep roots. As in India, Hinduism developed in layered forms in these islands too. What arrived from India was a fluid form of Hinduism in which Buddhist elements were also found. It then became synthesized with local cultural practices. The fluidity of this layered form is reflected in a traditional name for the religion "Siva-Buda" (referring to Shiva and the Buddha) in the Indonesian island of Bali where it still prevails as a majority religion followed by over 85% of residents. In other islands of Indonesia like Java and Sumatra, and in the neighboring countries like Cambodia and Thailand, Hinduism receded in the background as religion but still has deep cultural imprints discussed below.

Balinese Hinduism demands special attention not only because of its prevalence in the midst of other Indonesian islands that have been predominantly Islamic for several centuries but also because of the distinctive ways in which the synthesis of local worship practices with Vedic and Puranic Hinduism has vibrantly thrived in it. In Bali, the Hindu triad of Brahma, Vishnu, and Shiva finds recurrent references. But equally important in worship practices are various ancestral and nature spirits called *hyang*s. The Balinese Hindu belief in one Supreme Being called "Sang Hyang Acintya" combines the Balinese term *hyang* and the Sanskrit term *acintya* (inconceivable). It parallels Upanishadic Brahman and the Vedic concept of *ṛta* (cosmic order). Today, this theological concept also has political significance for Balinese Hindus, formally known in Indonesia as the followers of Agama Hindu Dharma. Since the 1950s, they have used the concept to represent themselves as monotheists in the Indonesian government framework where it is a requirement. In the areas of worship and life cycle rituals, festivals, social organization, and goals of life too, a weaving of Vedic, Puranic and local cultural elements is seen. Some festivals like the new year Nyegi have parallels to Hindu festivals in India such as Maharashtrian Gudi Padva (also new year). But others are distinctive to Bali and follow a completely different calendar of 210 days. One of these, Galungan, symbolizing victory of good over evil is celebrated with reflective and fasting practices and ends with processions of women carrying offerings of fruits arranged in exquisite arrangements. In art and architecture, the fluidity of lines and movements that marks the art of South-East Asia is seen dominantly in Balinese temples and sacred dances based on the epics and Puranas. Classification of social groups based on hereditary professions called *wangsa* parallels the *varṇa* system of ancient India but with greater flexibility. Thus, Balinese Hinduism demonstrates great resourcefulness and resilience of spirit. It draws on the spiritual resources of Hinduism for its needs but resists verbatim following of Indian models. In its distinctive form, it continues to thrive as a minority religion in Indonesia.

In other parts of South-East Asia, Hinduism no longer thrives as a religion. But its cultural imprints are grand in some respects; and vibrantly alive in art and popular culture. The largest sacred complex in the world, built in the twelfth century by Khmer king Suryavarman in the present-day Cambodia, Angkor Wat, presents the symbolism of Mount Meru (the mythical abode of Hindu deities) with exquisite carvings, even though it later developed as a

Buddhist site. This Khmer style temple is a UNESCO World Heritage site attracting tourists in large numbers. Similarly, the ninth-century Prambanan temple in Java, Indonesia, dedicated to the Hindu triad – Brahma, Vishnu, and Shiva (who is most prominent here) – is awestriking in grandeur. Despite being damaged recurrently because of natural disasters, it is well preserved by the Indonesian government. Bangkok airport in Thailand has an immense display of the Puranic myth of churning of the milky ocean. In performing arts, the narratives from the epics have formed main themes of the famous Indonesian shadow puppets, and dance drama genres based on the *Ramayana* prevail in several South-East Asian countries. Indeed, "The Ramayana festival" held in New Delhi in 2018 during the India–ASEAN commemorative summit included performances from Indonesia, Philippines, Thailand, Laos, and Cambodia. These imprints, which have long survived after Hinduism's disappearance as a religious tradition, point to the enduring appeal of the epic/Puranic narratives not only for Hindus, but also more broadly.

As the above brief survey of Hinduism's prevalence (not necessarily as a majority religion) in South and South-East Asia indicates, it has taken deep roots in regions where elements of classical Hinduism offer only one layer of religious life – whether through concepts, narratives, or divine figures. These get inextricably woven with layers of indigenous traditions and cultures, to ground the tradition deeply in the landscape. To an extent, these organic developments can be seen as a function of the absence of a central authoritative institution that could dispatch directives or ordinances from a far-off land.

CENTURIES OF DIASPORAS (NINETEENTH CENTURY ONWARD)

Hinduism's journey to various parts of the world in recent centuries has been very different from the above. Much of it has been through diaspora (i.e., group migration) with many different trajectories, leading to the tradition taking diverse forms in various contexts. A comprehensive survey of all its phases is not possible here, but we will look at a few major ones.

Indentured Labor

Some of the most challenging circumstances in which Hinduism was carried and transplanted in foreign lands was in the context of colonial rule when workers from India (belonging to diverse religious communities) were transported to other British colonies as indentured laborers, derogatively called "coolies." These were bonded laborers who were recruited to work on sugar and cotton plantations as well as building railway tracks, after slavery was abolished in British colonies in the early 1830s. In the following decades until WWI, India proved a storehouse of cheap labor because people who were greatly impoverished by recurrent famines desperately sought work. British recruiting agents found laborers who signed bonds to travel to colonies in Africa, the Caribbean islands of Trinidad and Tobago, Guyana (formerly British Guiana), Fiji, Mauritius, etc. Gaitura Bahadur's book *Coolie Woman*, which is based on extensive research as she attempted to trace her great grandmother's journey from India to Guyana, gives an illuminating account of the conditions in which indentured women and men embarked on a journey to unknown lands. Markers of their caste identities were removed before boarding the ship. Many died during long sea voyages and when they disembarked, all they could care for was survival in places whose language, people, seasons, foods, and landscapes were completely unfamiliar. Mostly uneducated, they carried few sacred texts and objects (Figure 7.2).

With little hope or even desire to return to the homeland, those who survived the harsh conditions of indentured labor settled in the colonies at the end of their bond periods. As they started to reconfigure their lives finding substitutes for familiar foods, clothing, and plants, they also began to reconstitute their religious lives, bonding over language (many recruits in a colony were from the same linguistic region) and religion rather than caste. Their building blocks were memory, songs, and fragmented pieces of their home religious ethos. Their resilience drew much on the power of songs — of saint-poets, women's, and folk — that they knew "by heart." A few generations later, the languages are forgotten but the songs are not. They are still sung zealously in Hindu communities

Figure 7.2 Indentured laborers in Trinidad.
Source: Wikimedia.

formed by descendants of indentured migrants. Among sacred texts, BG and saint-poet Tulsidas's Hindi *Ramayana* have been the pillars of their religious practices and social life. In 2015, I met a Hindu woman from Fiji in New Zealand who invited me to her home for dinner and for sharing her recitation of the *Ramayana*. Before touching the text, she took a bath to purify her body and put flowers near the book wrapped in a red silk scarf. Even though she did not know Hindi or Avadhi, she chanted a few passages in the same way I had heard them in India. She also proudly shared videos of *Rām-līlā* (the sacred theater form mentioned earlier) that her family has participated in for generations. She stated that for Fijian Hindus, the activities around the *Ramayana* anchor both their faith and their sociopolitical identity as a minority. The practices and important festivals among descendants of indentured laborers differ country to country depending on the place of origins of the community and the local contexts that shaped them. These also inevitably differ from those found in India. However, better financial conditions of the communities and accessibility of travel now allow many to visit India for pilgrimage and to invite religious experts and temple architects. These diverse forms in the global context parallel regional forms of Hinduism in India. Hindus form a thin majority in Mauritius (less than 50%) and a sizable minority (15–25%) in Fiji, Guyana, and Trinidad and Tobago.

Green Pastures

A few Hindus had started to migrate to England during the colonial period. Some of the royalties of princely states had built residences in England and many employees of the British army also chose to stay back. But Hindus in significant numbers began to arrive in the UK after WWII. As the colonies in Africa and elsewhere started to become independent, many British passport holders living in them saw it more beneficial to move to England. Many from Punjab who had lost everything during the partition also arrived here in the 1950s. These groups were not economically well-off, but were not as disadvantaged as the indentured laborers who were completely disoriented on arrival in their new homelands. The community, however, did face discrimination at times from politically and religiously conservative groups in the UK. Until the 1970s Hindus and other groups from South Asia and Africa worked together to voice resistance to discrimination, even using on one occasion the popular Hindu practice of *Rām-līlā* performance with reinterpretation and humor, as shown by Paula Richman's essay "The Ramayana in Southhall." Yet, the changing political scenes in South Asia have impacted collaborations in the diasporas too, especially in Europe and North America. Gradually Hindus have concentrated in some locations such as Wembley near London. Their growing economic strength allows them now to be more visually articulate. They have recently built temples in traditional styles, which also serve as social gathering places. The Swaminarayan temple in Neasden, London, completed in 1995 with traditional sculptures and pieces imported from India, has been nicknamed one of "the seven wonders of London," and has received recognition for its grandeur. Some second- and third-generation Hindus are also getting active on the political scene. A young Hindu, Rishi Sunak, has just become the Prime Minister of England.

The Hindu presence in North America has followed a different trajectory. As we have seen in the previous chapter, Swami Vivekananda and Paramhamsa Yogananda had established a positive image of Hinduism, almost as a counterculture among a section of Americans by the 1930s. Several Americans also traveled to India in the 1960s and became disciples of Hindu mystics like Neem Karoli Baba of the Himalayas. A large percentage of Hindu residents of the USA today, however, arrived there after the immigration laws amendments in 1965. Many of them were highly educated professionals – doctors, engineers, academics, lawyers – who soon became prosperous. Hindus have been arriving in large numbers in the USA since the 1980s, especially with the IT jobs opening. Because of the community's prosperity, several large traditional style temples (some belonging to specific sects) have been built in various parts of the country. Many trained priests and other experts have been invited. The continued growth of the community has also allowed some caste organizations to form. These provide platforms for community bonding, especially for the older generations. But they may or may not serve as effective networks for arranging marriages as expected, especially for the second- and third-generation Hindus who have grown up in the USA. There is a diversity of views on the importance of caste in marriage. Even though surveys indicate otherwise, in the past ten years, only one of about a dozen Hindu weddings I have attended in the USA was within a caste. Most were interfaith. The families of these couples seemed to view the USA as their home country and interfaith marriages as a channel for cultural integration. Other channels through which Hindus in the USA are striving to both preserve their cultural traditions and seek integration within the American ethos as contributors are schools of dance and music, public celebrations of festivals like Diwali, participation in interfaith initiatives, and engagement with the political scene. They have been successful to a degree. Yet, the journey is not always easy. Even with their considerable economic privilege, at times, Hindu communities in the USA have faced vandalism at their temples and slurs about practices. A parallel trajectory can also be seen in two oceanic aspirational destinations – Australia and New Zealand.

Even though with different trajectories, in the current times, diaspora Hindus worldwide share a crucial concern: transmission of the tradition to the next generation. Retaining the interest of younger generations is an issue faced by religious communities globally. But it is a daunting task in the diaspora for minority communities, especially with no formal traditional structure of religious education as in Hinduism. Hindu families and organizations are often sharply divided about the impact of representations of Hinduism in the global media and other discourses, especially those focusing on the issues of caste, gender, and religious nationalism in India and discussing them as present in the diaspora communities. Younger Hindus' questions about these sociopolitical issues have led communities to search for ways to transmit the tradition that adequately address them. Unlike the nineteenth-century leaders in India who were faced with questions raised by outsiders, these questions come from both outside and within. The urgency of the issue is unquestioned. But there prevail multiple views and animated/heated debates about it in print, virtual, and social media, as well as importantly, among friends and within families. These continue in the twenty-first century the age-old tradition of multivocality first seen in the Vedic texts.

EMBRACING HINDUISM IN WESTERN LANDS

Any account of Hinduism today remains incomplete without a brief introduction to relatively new Hindu communities that do not have ancestral ties with South Asia. Here, we will consider three such communities, each of which has distinctively contributed to Hinduism's global presence.

International Society of Krishna Consciousness

As we have seen, since the late nineteenth century, many Hindu ascetics and gurus have visited the West and have built large communities of disciples. Most of them have focused on the psychological aspects of inner transformation through eastern spiritual practices and have often invoked Christian and other faiths in their teachings. External markers of spiritual identity have not been required for their discipleship. But a notable exception to this trend was introduced by Swami Bhaktivedanta Prabhupad (1896–1977) in the late 1960s. Prabhupad, an ascetic in the Bengali Vaishnava tradition focused on Krishna worship called Gaudiya Vaishnavism, arrived in New York at the age of 69. It was during the Vietnam war. Many Americans were traveling to India in search of spiritual masters. After initial difficulties, Prabhupad found a few young disciples who not only became Krishna devotees, but also donned Indian ascetic attire, made Vaishnhava marks on foreheads, shaved their heads, and began chanting the mantra of Hare Krishna ecstatically on the streets of New York. This started a movement that came to be known as "Hare Krishna," whose official name is International Society of Krishna Consciousness (ISKCON). It was a distinctly missionary group that required adoption of Indian attire, vegetarianism, and other cultural markers for membership. Yet it was an American movement and not Indian. It grew rapidly in the early 1970s but was then entangled in controversies and court cases in the USA. The movement, however, did not come to an end. It has grown consistently and widely with temples and communities in Africa, Australia, and Europe including Russia and Ukraine whose members identify as Hindus. Many ISKCON communities celebrate their public ritual – the *rath yātra* (chariot procession) – with music and dance on the streets of their cities (Figure 7.3).

The most remarkable feature of their trajectory is that it is a Hindu movement rooted in a sixteenth-century devotional tradition of Bengal but was established in New York, spread worldwide, and now has several centers in India with non-Indian priests. A major center is in a town right next to the town of the 16th century mystic. ISKCON is respected in India as a Krishna devotion sect and its priests get due regard without consideration of race or caste. As a missionary current of Hinduism, it has extended the tradition's reach as a world religion and in the process, it has offered new dimensions to its worship structures.

Figure 7.3 Rath Yatra in the Moscow region, Russia, in winter (2011 year).
Courtesy: Creative Commons via Wikimedia.

The Saiva Siddhanta Church

Unlike ISKCON, founded by an Indian guru in the USA, the Saiva Siddhanta Church, a monastic institution rooted in the Shaiva yogic traditions of Sri Lanka, was founded by an American, who was born as Robert Hansen and later came to be known as Sivaya Subramuniyaswami (1927–2001). Hansen spent a few years as a youth with spiritual masters in Sri Lanka and advanced remarkably in yoga practices rooted in the Shaivite traditions there. He was given the title Subramuniya by Sri Lankan guru Yogaswami. On his return to the USA, Subramuniyaswami established the Saiva Siddhanta Church in 1949, formally incorporated in the State of California in 1957. The term "church" is interpreted broadly as "religious community" by the institution. The international head-quarter of the church was founded in Kaui Hawaii in 1970 and a center in Mauritius in 1981. The church also has householder members in many countries some of whom serve as missionaries for the spread of its teachings. The core teachings and practices of the church focus on self-realization through meditation, study of sacred texts, temple worship, *bhakti* toward the guru, and selfless service rooted in Shaivite Hinduism. Yet it also fosters alliances with other Hindu traditions. An important contribution of the institution that reaches literally thousands around the world is education about Hinduism through its online/print magazine *Hinduism Today*, published by its Himalayan Academy. The magazine provides a much-needed resource for the urgent issue of religious education of the younger generation mentioned earlier. Different in its missionary spirit from ISKCON, this institution too has helped Hinduism's reach to many corners of the world.

Hinduism in Ghana

As we have seen earlier, the British colonial presence in various parts of the world generated circuits of migrations of people unanticipated earlier. A circuit of this type on which thousands of Indians migrated to African countries like South Africa, Kenya, Tanzania, etc. is well known. But less known (except for Christian missionary work) are the unprecedented religious circuits created in the colonial context. Hinduism in Ghana can be seen at a node on such a circuit (Figure 7.4).

As per some scholars, Hindu worship practices were brought (not for propagation) to Ghana soon after WWI by Gujarati merchants with their worship of Lakshmi, goddess of wealth, during Diwali, which closely paralleled the worship of African water goddess Mami Wata. Ghanian religious imagination has a focus on miraculous powers of superhuman spirits. As per a belief, by traveling to far off magical lands, these spirits gain extra power that can be harnessed for sorcery, magic cures, etc. Gradually stories of Mami Wata carrying spirits to India, the land of Lakshmi and other powerful celestial beings, began circulating in Ghana, which are still alive. These were early precursors of the development of Hindu communities in the 1970s. According to scholar of Ghanian religion Albert Wuaku, however, the ground for the establishment of ISKCON and other forms of Hinduism in the 1970s was prepared more firmly by Ghanian soldiers in WWII who spent some time in

Figure 7.4 Hindus in Ghana celebrating Ganesh Chaturthi.
Photograph by Banksboomer, Courtesy: Wikimedia.

India. On their return, they served as spiritual healers using Hindu elements and told stories about the miraculous protective powers (*juju* in Ghanian vocabulary) of Hindu gods like Shiva and chants of OM. Other factors enhancing the appeal of Hinduism were Indian films with scenes of miracles, migration of some Hindus from Sindh after the partition of India, and magical shows by performers called "Professor Hindus."

After getting independence in 1957, Ghana went through a period of political instability for several years starting in the late 1960s.

The uncertainties about the future made room for the success of spiritual science groups that offered ways to develop mental powers to overcome adversities effectively. It was in this environment that Hindu Monastery of Africa (est. 1975) was established in Accra by Swami Ghanananda, a Ghanian who trained in Rishikesh, India. And the ISKCON center was established in 1979 through the influence of African American disciples of Swami Prabhupad. ISK-CON's missionary efforts have resulted in four important centers in southern Ghana and many small cells. Even though some Ghanians find ISKCON's stress on vegetarian diet and stress on detachment from worldly affairs (linking them to the global Hare Krishna community) as leading to a sort of aloofness from the local culture, overall, the tradition has stabilized in Ghana without Indianization as in other places. Swami Ghanananda's center benefited greatly

Table 7.1 Hinduism outside India

Historical context	*Geographical context*	*Present-day countries*	*Distinct features*
Until the end of the first millennium	South Asia	Sri Lanka, Nepal	Coexistence and to an extent fluidity with Buddhism
	South-East Asia	Bali	Woven with indigenous worship practices
Diaspora since the nineteenth century	British Colonies	Fiji, Guyana, African countries, Trinidad and Tobago	Indentured labor and retaining tradition in harsh circumstances
	Europe, North America, Oceania	UK, USA, Canada, Australia, and New Zealand	Post-colonial and professional migrations – affluence allowing traditional forms
New Hindu Currents	Global	Many countries	Propagation through teachings and missions of Hindu gurus from both India and other countries

from his charismatic personality. Today, they flourish along with other currents of Hinduism, making it a fast-growing religion in the country. The Ghanian forms of Hinduism (some of its newest) reinforce a pattern we have seen time and again in the exploration of the tradition in this book. They highlight that in the spread of Hinduism within or outside of India, the key has been its indigenization. While a degree of indigenization occurs in the spread of all traditions, it is made somewhat easy in the case of Hinduism because of the absence of a central authority. Indigenous cultures and aspirations offer the warp with which Hindu elements (thought or practice) get woven as woof.

FURTHER EXPLORATION SUGGESTIONS

Bahadur, Gaiutra. 2014. *Coolie Woman: The Odyssey of Indenture.* Chicago, IL: University of Chicago Press.

Bryant, Edwin, and Maria Ekstrand. 2004. *The Hare Krishna Movement: The Postcharismatic Fate of a Religious Transplant.* New York, NY: Columbia University Press.

Goldberg, Philip. 2010. *American Veda: From Emerson and the Beatles to Yoga and Meditation: How Indian Spirituality Changed the West.* New York, NY: Harmony Books.

Kurien, Prema A. 2007. *A Place at the Multicultural Table: The Development of an American Hinduism.* Piscataway, NJ: Rutgers University Press.

Paramacharya Sadasivanathaswami ed. 1979–. *Hinduism Today.* Kapaa, HI: The Himalayan Academy. Accessed August 14, 2022. https://www.hinduismtoday.com/.

Public Broadcasting Associates. 1981. *The Three Worlds of Bali.* (Videocassette.) Watertown, MA: Documentary Educational Resources.

Richman, Paula. "A Diaspora Ramayana in Southall, Greater London." *Journal of the American Academy of Religion* 67, no. 1 (1999): 33–57. Accessed August 14, 2022. http://www.jstor.org/stable/1466032.

Wuaku, Albert Kafui. 2013. *Hindu Gods in West Africa: Ghanaian Devotees of Shiva and Krishna.* Leiden: Brill

EPILOGUE

Having surveyed layered historical, spatial, textual, ideological, social, and practice aspects of the tradition known to the world as "Hinduism," we can return to our initial consideration of the "-ism" part. We have looked at not only some of its strengths but also issues of severe social injustice that have prevailed in the Hindu society historically. We have seen that "Hinduism" indeed has many features of a religious system – sacred literature, schools of philosophy and theology, places of pilgrimage, worship rituals, etc. But is there a "religion" called "Hinduism"? With its immense diversity and the absence of a single sacred text, founder, required belief, or central authority can it be understood in the same way as traditions like Christianity or Islam? The answers to such questions, as we have seen throughout our survey, are not straightforward.

In recent decades, there have been many questions internally and from outside about the term "Hinduism," coined over 200 years ago. It is not a term people had been using for what they were following. It became gradually accepted in the nineteenth century by a large section of the community that was later formally classified as Hindu (followers of "Hinduism") in the census of British India. The implications of this identification were significantly different

DOI: 10.4324/9781315303352-9

from its ancient usage by Persians or the early modern usage of the term "Hindu." Since its inception, the term "Hinduism" has had a layer of political meanings. During the colonial period, the terms "Hinduism" and "Hindu" stirred both aggressive and defensive responses in public discourses and nationalist movements. In current times, in the democratic nation state of India, the terms still remain contested with political implications. Do all people classified as Hindu identify as such? Within India, a significant percentage of them do and a few do not. Some of them say they never have. Yet clusters of shared practices such as the worship of a family goddess or festivals like that of Ganesha or the goddess in a region regularly bring together people who do and do not identify as Hindu. On the other hand, those who identify as Hindus continue to engage in shared practices like veneration of saints with local Muslims or other religious communities. Outside of India, Hindus integrate several local/regional practices in their religious life. In these scenarios – are the practices or the people "Hindu"? People would certainly have different views.

What would a practicing Hindu say about being classified along with specific groups at one time and being separated from them at another? What would she say about the periodic naming, unnaming, and renaming of her identity and her religion? Perhaps, when confronted with questions about religion and identity, a practicing Hindu would say with a smile, "Call me and my religion what you may!" She would perhaps be thinking at the moment that beyond the political implications of naming and renaming, what she follows is not a nicely packaged "ism," but a dharmic orientation that allows her to draw elements from diverse sources. These include ancient texts and concepts filtered through vernacular songs, encounters with other cultures, and contemporary currents of ethical thought. She would be cognizant at some level that in these, some components of her religious life are woven in patterns shared with diverse Hindu communities worldwide. But she would have confidence that it still remains rooted uncompromisingly in her local culture. Using the commonly heard term in her religious culture, *nām-rūpa* (name and form), she may point out that the labels are of little importance compared to the experience of approaching the sacred in whatever way one chooses. In support of her point, she may sing a few lines from a song of a saint-poet from her region. If it is Jashoda, she would perhaps sing the following lines from a popular song of the beloved saint-poet of her region Narasinha Mehta (translation mine), which not only suggests non-duality between the divine and the creation but also the relevance of multiple ways of worshiping.

> In the entire universe, it is only you, Śrī Hari (the resplendent, the Divine)!
> Limitless in your different forms.
> .. . .
> The Vedas pronounce and śāstras testify:
> "There is no distinction between gold and an earring.
> After styling, jewelry has different names and forms (nām-rūpa).
> In the end, it is all gold."
> [Religious scholars] created confusion with books, and did not tell the truth.
> Each one worships whom she/he adores.

For her, the freedom in the matters of worship would perhaps be the most important "basic" of "Hinduism." Such responses are not just likely; they are commonly encountered in actual conversations. They lead us to reflect again on the nature and basics of what we know as "Hinduism." Is it a religion, a culture, or an orientation? The survey in this work may lead some of us to see it as one or the other. Some may think that like other religious traditions of the world, it is all of them. But most would agree that a distinctive basic of it is its "multilayeredness" (if one can use such a term) in sacred texts, divine pantheon, worship practices, social customs, and arts with one layer firmly rooted in an indigenous culture. Not bound by one exclusively authoritative text or founding figure (except in sectarian forms), the diverse but overlapping currents of Hinduism continue to converge to make an enormous flow of religion like its namesake river Sindhu.

BIBLIOGRAPHY

ADDITIONAL SUGGESTED RESOURCES (ORGANIZED THEMATICALLY)

ANCIENT INDIA AND SACRED SANSKRIT TEXTS

O'Flaherty, Wendy Doniger. 1973. *Siva: The Erotic Ascetic*. Oxford: Oxford University Press.

Olivelle, Patrick. 2009. *The Law Code of Manu*. Oxford World's Classics. Oxford: Oxford University Press.

Thapar, Romila. 2003. *Early India: From the Origins to Ad 1300*. Berkeley, CA: University of California Press.

VERNACULAR TEXTS

Lalla, *Naked Song*. 1993. trans. Coleman Barks. Athens, GA: Maypop Books.

Lorenzen, David N. 1996. *Praises to a Formless God: Nirguṇī Texts from North India*. Suny Series in Religious Studies. Albany, NY: State University of New York Press.

Martin, Nancy. 1999. "Mīrābāī: Inscribed in Text, Embodied in Life." *Vaiṣṇavī Women and the Worship of Krishna*. Delhi: Motilal Banarasidass. 7–46.

Novetzke, Christian Lee. 2008. *Religion and Public Memory: A Cultural History of Saint Namdev in India*. New York: Columbia University Press.

Pollock, Sheldon. 1998. "India in the Vernacular Millennium: Literary Culture and Polity, 1000–1500." *Daedalus* 127, no. 3: 41–74. http://www.jstor.org/stable/20027507.

Richman, Paula. 1991. *Many Rāmāyaṇas: The Diversity of a Narrative Tradition in South Asia*. Berkeley, CA: University of California Press.

Shapiro Hawley, Nell, and Sohini Pillai. eds. 2021. *Many Mahābhāratas*. Albany, NY: State University of New York Press.

Singh, K.S. 1994. *Mahabharata in the Tribal and Folk Traditions of India*. Shimla: Indian Institute of Advanced Studies.

Singh, K. S., and Birendranatha Datta. 1993. *Rama-Katha in Tribal and Folk Traditions of India: Proceedings of a Seminar*. Calcutta: Anthropological Survey of India.

CASTE AND SOCIAL ORGANIZATION

Bidner, Chris, and Mukesh Easwaran. 2015. "A Gender-Based Theory of the Origin of the Caste System of India." *Journal of Development Economics* 114: 142–158. https://doi.org/10.1016/j.jdeveco.2014.12.006.

Carman, John Braisted, and Apffel-Marglin Frédérique. 1985. *Purity and Auspiciousness in Indian Society*. Leiden, Netherlands: E.J. Brill.

Das, Veena. 1968. "A Sociological Approach to the Caste Puranas: A Case Study." *Sociological Bulletin* 17, no. 2: 141–164. http://www.jstor.org/stable/23619308.

Deliege, Robert. 1993. "The Myths of Origin of the Indian Untouchables." *Man* 28, no. 3: 533–549. https://doi.org/10.2307/2804238.

Dumont, Louis. 1970. *Homo Hierarchicus: An Essay on the Caste System*. Translated by R. M. Sainsbury. Chicago, IL: University of Chicago Press.

Krishnan, Y. 1986. "Buddhism and Caste System." *The Journal of the International Association of Buddhist Studies* 9, no. 1: 71–84.

Olivelle, Patrick. 1998. "Caste and Purity: A Study in the Language of Dharma Literature." *Contributions to Indian Sociology* 32: 189–216.

Srinivas, Mysore Narasimhachar. 1966. *Social Change in Modern India*. Berkeley, CA: University of California Press.

WOMEN

Kumar, Radha. 1993. *The History of Doing: An Illustrated Account of Movements for Women's Rights and Feminism in India, 1800–1990*. London: Verso.

Shukla-Bhatt, Neelima. 2015. "Celebrating Materiality: Garbo, a Festival Image of the Goddess in Gujarat" in *Sacred Matters: Material Religion in*

South Asian Traditions edited by Tracy Pintchman and Corinne G. Dempsey. Albany, NY: State University of New York Press.

PHILOSOPHY AND ETHICS

Gupta, Bina. 2021. *An Introduction to Indian Philosophy: Perspectives on Reality, Knowledge, and Freedom.* Abingdon, UK: Routledge. https://doi.org/10.4324/9780429345210.

Martin, Nancy M. 2003. "Rights, Roles, and Reciprocity in Hindu Dharma" in *Human Rights and Responsibilities in World Religions* edited by Joseph Runzo, Nancy M. Martin and Arvind Sharma. Oxford: Oneworld.

Nadkarni, M.V. 2011. "Ethics in Hinduism" in *Ethics for Our Times: Essays in Gandhian Perspective.* Delhi: Oxford. https://doi.org/10.1093/acprof:oso/9780198073864.003.0010.

Perrett, Roy W. 1998. *Hindu Ethics: A Philosophical Study.* Honolulu, HI: University of Hawaii Press.

PRACTICES

Eck, Diana L. 1981. "India's 'Tīrthas': 'Crossings' in Sacred Geography," *History of Religions* 20, no. 4: 323–344. http://www.jstor.org/stable/1062459.

Eliade, Mircea. 1969. *Yoga: Immortality and Freedom.* translated from the French by Willard R. Trask. Princeton, NJ: Princeton University Press.

Michell, George. 1977. *The Hindu Temple: An Introduction to Its Meaning and Forms.* New York: Harper & Row.

Ranade, Ashok D. 2008. *Perspectives on Music: Ideas and Theories.* New Delhi: Promilla & Co.

HINDUISM IN MODERN TIMES

Baird, Robert D., ed. 2001. *Religion in Modern India.* New Delhi: Manohar Publishers & Distributors.

Husken, Ute, Vasudha Narayanan, and Astrid Zotter, eds. 2022. *Nine Nights of Power: Durgā, Dolls, and Darbārs.* Albany, NY: State University of New York Press.

Jain, Kajri. 2007. *Gods in the Bazaar: The Economies of Indian Calendar Art.* Durham, NC: Duke University Press.

Roy, Haimanti. 2018. *The Partition of India.* New Delhi, India: Oxford University Press.

Schultz, Anna C. 2013. *Singing a Hindu Nation: Marathi Devotional Performance and Nationalism.* New York: Oxford University Press.

Shukla-Bhatt, Neelima, 2014. "The Leap of the Limping Goddess: Ai Khodiyar of Gujarat" in *Inventing and Reinventing the Goddess* edited by Sree Padma. Lanham, MD: Lexington Books.

Yogananda, Paramahansa, and W. Y. Evans-Wentz. 1981. *Autobiography of a Yogi*. 12th ed. Los Angeles, CA: Self-Realization Fellowship.

HINDUISM BEYOND INDIA

Eisenlohr, Patrick. 2006. *Little India: Diaspora, Time, and Ethnolinguistic Belonging in Hindu Mauritius*. Berkeley, CA: University of California Press.

Hawker, Frances, Putu Resi, and Bruce Campbell. 2014. *Hinduism in Bali. Families and Their Faiths*. Carcroft, UK: Tulip Books.

Joshi, Khyati Y. 2006. *New Roots in America's Sacred Ground: Religion, Race, and Ethnicity in Indian America*. New Brunswick, NJ: Rutgers University Press.

Rambachan, Anantanand, and Brian A. Hatcher. 2016. *Hinduism in Fiji, Mauritius, South Africa, and Trinidad*. Religions in the Modern World. New York: Routledge.

INTERNET SOURCES

Bindu. 2021. "Rig Veda Chanting | Vedic Mantras | Vol 1–3" by Flammen-Quelle. Video: 2:13:59. https://www.youtube.com/watch?v=lW5W-ByctPsw. Accessed December 5, 2022.

BYU MOA. 2015. "Hindu Temple Worship—BYU Museum of Art – Loving Devotion." Video: 4:00. https://www.youtube.com/watch?v=qP2ZMJAqUts. Accessed December 5, 2022.

Hindu Pilgrimage Destinations. https://www.tourmyindia.com/pilgrimage/hindu-pilgrimage-tour.html. Accessed December 4, 2022.

Mata, Amritanandmayi. https://amma.org/. Accessed December 5, 2022.

Sana, Amjad. 2022. "Diwali Celebration in Pakistan 2022 | HAPPY DIWALI." Video: 18:56. https://www.youtube.com/watch?v=0_NOO1GoMn4. Accessed December 5, 2022.

Sanskrit Sacred Texts. https://sanskritdocuments.org/. Accessed December 4, 2022.

INDEX

Bold page numbers indicate tables, *italic* numbers indicate figures.